P9-DCS-111

LIVING
DANGEROUSLY

A Behind the Scenes Look at
The Climate Change Debate

RICK
JOYNER

MorningStar Publications

LIVING

DANGEROUSLY

Living Dangerously
by Rick Joyner
Copyright ©2014

Distributed by MorningStar Publications, Inc.,
a division of MorningStar Fellowship Church
375 Star Light Drive, Fort Mill, SC 29715

www.MorningStarMinistries.org
1-800-542-0278

Unless otherwise indicated, all Scripture quotations are taken from the New American Standard Bible, copyright © 1960, 1962, 1963, 1968, 1971, 1973, 1974, 1977 by The Lockman Foundation. Italics in Scripture are for emphasis only.

No part of this book may be reproduced or transmitted in any form or by any means, electronic, or mechanical, including photocopying, recording, or by any information storage and retrieval system, without written permission from the author.

All rights reserved.
Printed in the United States of America.

Cover and Layout Design: Kandi Evans

ISBN— 978-1-60708-569-0; 1-60708-569-0

Table of Contents

This much we do know: What we do to nature directly reflects our attitude toward our God who created and inhabits it.

– John Sandford, *Healing the Earth*

Introduction

Climate change is one of the biggest debates of our time. If climate change is happening and it is man caused, then it is one of the most important issues of our time. If it is not happening, or is not man caused, it is still one of the most important issues of our time because it is the most important ruse of our time. Either way, it has some of the most far-reaching consequences of any issue with which the world is now grappling.

As Jesus exhorted His followers to understand the signs of the times better than they understand the signs of weather, every Christian has a basic responsibility to understand the great issues of our time. Many of the ultimate issues that mankind is now facing are being drawn to the same crossroads around the issue of climate change. This book is written to condense and illuminate these issues.

This work is about my journey to understand climate change. My goal was to determine if it was real. If it was real, then I wanted to understand the consequences. If it wasn't real, I wanted to understand the agenda of those who were propagating it. I learned far more than I expected. The implications of this are more far reaching than I ever imagined.

We will examine the main factors in this climate change debate from both sides of the issue. I have sought to do this objectively, and I think I have been in a good position to be objective. Even though I entered this journey as a climate change skeptic, I have no compelling reason to believe in climate change or not to believe in it. I just did not want to be convinced of anything like this without clear evidence. If climate change is true, I want to know it, and I want to understand the implications. If it is not true, it is of the upmost importance that we understand who is promoting this and why it is being used in this way.

Like many complex issues of our time, I found merit on both sides of this debate. Those who think there is no merit to the other side's argument have likely based their position on propaganda and may not really understand the issue. There is also a lot of distortion and misinformation on both sides. Our goal should be to understand the issue in a way that will lead us to the right conclusion and the proper actions in response to it. However, we will find that this is about much more than climate change.

Those who do not understand the important issues of our time are ruled by those who do. Climate change is an important issue, and it is now being used to control much of our lives. The trend is for it to take an increasing amount of control. Whether it deserves this control over us or not is a crucial issue that will affect us all. Every responsible person should seek to understand it.

High-impact people in every age are those who do not run from controversy but rather to it, knowing that the issue would not be controversial if it were not important. We must be willing to push through the fog that surrounds this issue or something very deadly could be growing that will be too big for us to deal with by the time we do see it.

The informed are the forearmed. They are the ones who win the great debates of the times. Even so, we should not want to win a debate when we are on the wrong side. Above all things, we should want the truth to be the victor.

My journey to understand this issue illuminated so many things that are already having a major impact on every one of us. I realize that few have the time or opportunity to take such a journey, so this book is written to condense thousands of hours of research and many varied and remarkable experiences about climate change and related subjects into what you can absorb in just a few hours.

I have not written this to convince you of my conclusions, though I will share them with you. Coming to the right conclusions about the issue of climate change is important, but far more important is gaining the knowledge and understanding that will help us to discern the truth about this and many other issues as well. This leads to wisdom, which is the ability to see the truth and to apply the knowledge of the truth correctly.

This book is written for open, thinking people who live with the courage to want to know the truth and have the resolve to stand for truth regardless of the consequences.

1

The Most Important Story

"This is the most important story of our times," filmmaker James Cameron said in the extraordinary documentary on climate change, *Years of Living Dangerously*. Produced by Cameron, Arnold Schwarzenegger, and Jerry Weintraub, this project brought together some of the biggest stars in Hollywood, world renowned scientists, correspondents, dignitaries, and my daughter and I.

So why would I, a white, Southern, conservative, evangelical, pastor, and climate change skeptic, along with his daughter, an environmental activist and true believer in man-made climate change, be asked to be a part of this documentary?

You are probably thinking what I did. This is either to make me look as foolish and out of touch as possible, thereby humiliating others who share my position, or to document my conversion into believing in man-made climate change. These were likely the original intent, but the outcome was different and quite unexpected.

Thinking about the title they had chosen for this project, I thought that I would be the one living dangerously. Unless I became a climate change convert, I could see no positive result for me to be a part of this. Even so, I had a personal motto that I might die of a lot of things, but boredom was not going to be one of them. Like many things that are dangerous, I felt that this was a greater opportunity than what it seemed on the surface. This turned out to be very true.

I also wanted to know the truth about man-made climate change, but I would not be a cheap convert. I don't think we can be, if we really care about the truth. Even more importantly, for over forty years I have lived my life following what I call "God trails." These are like adventures He leads us on to find the great treasures of knowledge and understanding. I knew this was one, but like all of the others, it would be strewn with dangers. What makes something a treasure is either that it is rare or hard to get to. The greater the treasure, the more rare it is and the more difficult it is to attain. This one was hard, but it was well worth it.

The Journey Begins

As stated, I was a man-made climate change skeptic when we began work on this documentary but not a denier, and there is a difference. The main challenge I had with believing in climate change was the hysteria surrounding it. In my sixty-five years, I have learned that truth has a certain dignity, a grace that is strong and does not have to be reactionary or established by exaggerations. On the surface, the climate change position had all of the indicators pointing to it being a major exaggeration, at best.

I also know how partial truths are often grasped partially by superficial or extreme people who muddy the waters for everyone else. True, biblical Christianity has been one of the biggest victims of this, so I try not to completely embrace or discount an issue until I have time to do the required research. I had to give climate change a chance.

My main challenges with man-made climate change were spiritual, moral, psychological, political, mathematical, and scientific. I have a level of knowledge, education, and experience in each of these. The basic manner in which the climate change argument was being presented pointed to not just problems in all of these areas, but major problems. This leads to other issues. Even if climate change is real, those presently driving the narrative are likely reactionary, and how they manage the problem is likely distorted. If climate change is true, it seemed that the truth was in the wrong hands.

Many of the pro-climate change articles I read I considered an insult to an intelligent, knowledgeable thinker. However, that may not be the readers' fault. Winston Churchill once said, "The best argument against democracy is a five-minute conversation with the average voter." Most people do not have time to seek a deeper understanding of the many and varied important issues of our time. Therefore, superficial arguments and articles can have a great impact, so you can't blame the proponents for using these. For this reason, those who do want to understand the issues must go beyond what the media presents.

Even though my objections included the areas listed above, I knew the only way to really settle the issue of climate change was mathematical and scientific. The other issues are issues, and they are muddying the waters, but the issue of man-made climate change could be proven or disproven by math and science. When I was told that if I participated in this documentary I would be able to dialog with some of the top scientists in the world, it was an opportunity I could not pass up.

During the year that we worked on this project I had many of my questions answered. Many were answered that I had not even asked or knew to ask. That is why I love these adventures! I learned far more than I expected. Some of these were "ultimate questions," crucial for understanding much more than climate change—they are about the times in which we live and the basic condition of the world at this time.

This is why I am presenting this information in a way that can address many critical issues, as well as bring some understanding to the issues around climate change. These will be easy for you to grasp even if you are not good at math or science. As Christians, we also have an unfair advantage—the One who created math and science is our Teacher.

I have done substantial research on the science and math, as well as the political, psychological, and economic consequences of this issue. To include all of my sources here would require this book to be many times the size it is, even many more volumes. For this reason, I have provided my source studies on a website so that you can download the articles and studies that interest you at your convenience. You will find the link for these sources at the end of Chapter 10.

Again, I tried to be as objective as possible in my study. However, a truly objective study is rare and maybe non-existent, regardless of what the author(s) may claim. So this is presented as a subjective but accurate narrative. We can be subjective and still be true. I have not intentionally distorted or tried to color anything, but I also understand that we all have filters. For the sake of integrity, I will be candid about factors that may have colored my perspective on these issues and let you be the judge.

This includes an account of the making of this documentary, *Years of Living Dangerously.* I think you will find these interesting, but they also include crucial insights into how our culture is being shaped and how most of the information that is now presented through the media is shaped.

Even though this is a subjective narrative, I did not want to be speculative, especially about anyone's motives, unless it can be substantiated. As Christians, we have a biblical responsibility to think the best of others, as we are commanded in I Corinthians 13. Because of this, it is my resolve to assume good motives on the part of others until it is proven otherwise. This can seem naïve to the critical and cynical, and it can be. That being understood, I have learned that the cynical are far more likely to be deceived. For this reason, we are called to live by faith and not by fear.

I am also experienced enough to know that people can have the best motives yet still be profoundly deceived or profoundly wrong in their application of the truth. Personally, I don't like conspiracy theories or the paranoia that surrounds them. However, as the saying goes, "just because you are paranoid does not mean someone is not after you." There are conspiracies and agendas. History is littered with their devastation when they are not recognized and exposed early. Just because I don't like conspiracy theories and don't spend time looking for them, I do always try to keep my antennas up.

As a Christian and ministry leader, I have learned a lot about deception and how to discern it. I have learned to trust that evil intent will ultimately be exposed under scrutiny. I have learned to trust the Holy Spirit to lead me into all truth and to have more faith in Him than in the enemy to deceive me. Therefore, I don't fear treading in places where few Christians will go, but I do so with respect for the dangers.

President Reagan once said after signing a nuclear reduction treaty with the Soviets, "We will trust, but verify." Suspicion is not a fruit of the Holy Spirit, so I refuse to be guided by it. However, I also believe it is a basic job of the Holy Spirit to uncover and reveal, so I seek to be open to all that is revealed. I was surprised by how active He was in this project and the importance of what He is revealing through the whole climate change cause.

That being said, again, on the surface the man-made climate change position has many signs that are typical of a ruse. For this reason, I approached it with my guard up, probably more than usual. What I found surprised me and can be a major factor in helping us understand these times. I also consider some of this understanding to be necessary for navigating through what is unfolding. I think these insights will benefit you regardless of where you are or where you land on climate change.

2

Foundations

In this narrative, I am going to include some of my background and experience to be as candid as I can about my perspective. These are also included because they have insights into this debate on climate change and other major issues that are related.

When I was young, I was a spiritual, moral, social, and political radical. I am sixty-five years old at this writing, and I am still a radical in all of these. When I was young, I was radical because it fit my rebellious personality. Now I am radical because I became a follower of the most radical Teacher to ever walk the earth—Jesus. He was a Radical, but not a rebel, and there can be a difference. Jesus was the Truth. The truth is radical. When truth is presented, it will shake and threaten anything that is not built on it. That is why all who seek the truth will always be controversial, which is another word for "threatening the status quo."

Radical means "basic." Basics, or fundamentals, are critical to every discipline, endeavor, or field of knowledge. This is why the most successful in every field are those who do the basics best. When I seek to understand something, I try to find the foundations it is built on. That is what I mean by being a radical. However, in these times of increasing information and knowledge, but also with increasing shallowness, doing anything with much depth will be perceived as radical.

That being said, I don't want to stand on the side of conservatives or liberals, but on the side of truth. If that leads me to be conservative in some areas and liberal in others, then so be it. My resolve is to find the truth. After that, my resolve is to stand for the truth, regardless of the consequences. That is how my Teacher lived, and that is how I seek to live.

Even though I consider myself a radical, in fairness to the present understanding of people, most would call me a spiritual, moral, social, and political conservative. Many of the conservative positions are the radical, or basic, positions that both our faith and nation, the United States, were built upon.

While understanding this, I try to never forget that it was the religious and political conservatives who had the greatest hope in the coming of the Messiah, but were the worst enemies of the Messiah when He came. So it is my resolve to never take a position just because it is conservative or liberal, but because it is right. We are told in I Corinthians 2:10, "**For to us God revealed** *them* **through the Spirit; for the Spirit searches all things, even the depths of God.**" Therefore, no one who follows the Spirit will be shallow. It is often the shallow who base their beliefs on partial information or understanding and are misled by bad agendas.

As we are also told in this Scripture, "**the Spirit searches all things,**" not just religious things, but even issues like climate change. We are in need today of those like Daniel who excel in every field of wisdom and knowledge. Because of Daniel's love and respect for God, he may have been one of the most learned men of his time, but he lived with a remarkable humility That humility is required for those who would discern truth.

In I Corinthians 13, we read that we "see in part, prophesy in part, and know in part." So no one has the complete picture. To have the whole picture, we need to put what we understand together with what others have. Understanding comes from *standing under* someone else's position. The greatest understanding can come from seeking to understand those we may disagree with.

For the most part, conservatives already have the perspective I have, so I try to hear and understand the positions of others who are not in my circle. The fearful consider this dangerous, but I think it is more dangerous to not listen to the other side of a debate. This may confirm our beliefs or enhance them, but a major advantage of doing this is to gain perspectives and information we may not have, as well as the understanding that gives us an ability to discourse intelligently with those we disagree with.

We should have more faith in the Holy Spirit to lead us into all truth than we have in the enemy to deceive us, but as the Scripture exhorts, neither should we be ignorant of the enemy's schemes (see II Corinthians 2:11). If we do not have faith to go into something, we should stay out of it. I may have faith to go into some things that others don't, while others may have faith to go into things I don't. For this reason, I will be thankful that I can learn from you about them. That is one of the great advantages of being a part of the greatest society on earth—the body of Christ. That is why the Apostle Paul did not say, "*I* have the mind of Christ," but "*we* **have the mind of Christ**" **(see I Corinthians 2:16).** It takes all of us together to have His mind. We need each other.

Even if you are a Christian, I don't expect you to believe everything I say just because I'm a Christian. We should emulate the Bereans in the Book of Acts. Luke wrote that they were more noble-minded because they listened to the great Apostle Paul with an open mind, but then went back and searched the Scriptures to verify what he said. To verify what we will accept as truth is noble, and desperately needed, especially in these times. Today with the abundance of knowledge about everything so easily available from so many sources, the beliefs of many about some of the most important issues are based on "sound bites."

If you disagree with any of my positions, I would never want you to compromise your convictions. We must build our beliefs on verifiable truth. In the case of climate change, true science is required for verifiable truth. True science and true scientists are more rare than we may think. True science never approaches research seeking to prove something, but rather to discover the facts and let those facts lead where they may. For this reason, true science and true Christians should be best friends and allies. They are both in pursuit of the truth and are, for this reason, under assault from the superficial.

The tactics of some climate change zealots are a major reason for the growing skepticism around this issue. Skepticism about it is growing around the world, regardless of how the proponents will dispute this. However, history teaches us that this happens with virtually every truth. We must resolve not to discount an issue just because of the extremists. This is a reason for caution, but not rejection. We have our own zealots who do the same with most of the truth we hold dear.

The Tone

Some of the emerging generation admitted to siding with conservatives on most issues. With studies showing that 85% of teachers and professors leaned toward being liberals, 65% of students leaned toward being conservatives. The reason most students who leaned this way did not want to be identified as conservatives was because they cannot bear the tone they hear coming from conservatives.

Immature, arrogant, or mean-spirited people who have the truth can do the most damage to that truth. This tone has probably done far more damage to conservative causes than the opposition. It has been summed up that conservatives think that liberals are stupid, and liberals think that conservatives are mean. As shocking as this may be to conservatives, most people will follow stupid before mean. However, just about everyone would like to follow intelligence that is accompanied by humility and grace.

Granted, the tone now coming from liberals has become even harsher, but trumping each other with harshness is not going to lead us to the answers we need. When there is zeal with maturity, it will have an easy to perceive dignity and respect for others in its demeanor. In possibly the greatest biblical exhortation about discernment, James 3:13-18, we are told:

Who *is* wise and understanding among you? Let him show by good conduct *that* his works *are done* in the meekness of wisdom.

But if you have bitter envy and self-seeking in your hearts, do not boast and lie against the truth.

This wisdom does not descend from above, but *is* earthly, sensual, demonic.

For where envy and self-seeking *exist,* confusion and every evil thing *are* there.

But the wisdom that is from above is first pure, then peaceable, gentle, willing to yield, full of mercy and good fruits, without partiality and without hypocrisy.

Now the fruit of righteousness is sown in peace by those who make peace (NKJV).

Even though there may not seem to be much of this kind of magnanimity with many now promoting climate change, I found some on this journey. To my great surprise, I found it in places and with people I did not expect. I took this as needed reproof to my own prejudice.

There is a lot of clamor, and even hysteria, with some promoting climate change, but there are also voices of reason. Likewise there are raging deniers who sometimes fling extreme and false accusations about climate change believers. Even so, among skeptics and deniers, there are voices of reason too. Those are who we need to hear on both sides of this issue.

It's About Life

Before I became a Christian, I believed in the cause of protecting the environment. I was at the first Earth Day and have grown in my love of the environment the longer I've lived. I still consider myself an environmentalist, but now I'm one because I am a Christian. Of all people, Christians should be the most devoted environmentalists. The first command given to man was to take care of the garden he was in, and that is still a basic human responsibility. This is such an important issue with the Lord that we are told in Revelation 11:17-18 that when the Lord returns to reign over the earth, He will **"destroy those who destroy the earth."**

The Lord so loved the *world* that He gave His Son for its redemption. If we are doing anything to seriously threaten this planet, we must investigate it with the utmost concern and determination to find the truth, not just what we want to believe or what fits our own political agenda.

We must seek to know the truth regardless of how commercially or politically expedient it may or may not be. We should consider it a terrible failure to leave this earth in worse shape than it was before we lived because of what we did or failed to do. This is a major reason why I gave time and effort to understand this issue, and I intend to do more.

I am also appalled by the sometimes ruthless, shortsighted, misguided, and foolish extremes in the environmental movement. Even though it may seem this movement is overloaded with such people, they are, unfortunately, to be found in almost every movement. If this could alone negate a cause, it would negate our own Christian faith. Environmental extremists hurt their cause, and we should never give in to the extremists. However, we also owe much to the environmental movement for the rivers and lands they have helped clean up and the species they have helped to save.

How can we be pro-life and not be for all life? The Lord does love people more than sparrows, but He loves sparrows too. We should be thankful for much of what the environmental movement has accomplished. We should also be thankful for our conservative friends who have helped to hold the extremes at bay and have prevented more human tragedies by the thoughtless application of their tactics.

Could it be possible for the environmental and conservative movements to link up? It is not only possible, it is happening. Bridges of trust are being built, and should be. The Great Commission to "go into all the world" was not just geographical. Christians should be engaged in every major field of knowledge and influence, with their influence being the salt and light they are called to be. Without salt and light provided by mature Christians, the extremes on both sides will continue to stir up and muddy the waters to the detriment of us all.

3

Thinking With Your Heart

James Cameron said that this documentary, *Years of Living Dangerously*, was "a people story." It was mostly about people and how they have been impacted by crises in the environment. There was not much science included, except a few charts and studies quoted that verified their predetermined position about climate change. Even so, this was not intended to be a documentary on whether climate change was real or not. The producers were already convinced of this. Therefore, *Years of Living Dangerously* was about how people have been impacted by a changing environment, and the changing environment is presumably caused by climate change.

Like it or not, this strategy is effective for introducing a subject or cause. Being emotionally engaged is usually necessary before people will get motivated to actually do something. However, when this is done deceptively, we must recognize it and reject it. Propaganda is built on the understanding that most people make decisions based on what they feel more than what they think. So if you are trying to persuade the average person, this way is effective. However, if you are trying to persuade high-impact people, this will often backfire.

A Family Matter

My oldest daughter, Anna Jane Joyner, is becoming a well-known environmental activist. I don't know anyone who is more passionate about saving the planet. We have our disagreements on some of this, especially on strategy and tactics, but I'm very proud of her and greatly appreciate her devotion. She will stand with great courage for what she believes, will take on some of the biggest issues, and fight some of the biggest opponents, armed with very little except for her belief that she is doing the right thing. This gives me great hope for her and the future.

The episode of this documentary (Episode 4) that features Anna and myself starts by building on the conflict between Anna Jane and myself about climate change. I understand that drama helps make a story interesting, but I was not happy with the inaccuracies that were portrayed about our relationship.

For example, it was said that I stopped paying Anna's tuition for a semester of college because she had started to believe in climate change. It is true that I did not pay her tuition for a semester, but it had nothing to do with her belief in climate change, or any other beliefs she had about the environment. In fact, I later subsidized Anna's income so that she could work for the Sierra Club.

It was then stated in *Years of Living Dangerously* that Anna and I did not speak to each other for six months. That never happened. I have never cut off communication to any of my children for a single moment. I would not do such a thing. Neither have they ever cut off communication with me. Like all families, we have differences. However, cutting off communication by any of us, for any reason, is something I cannot imagine. This was very disappointing to see injected into this documentary.

Then the conclusion of our episode made it look like, in the end, I had been at least persuaded enough about climate change to let Anna Jane address our congregation on the subject. The truth is, I have allowed Anna to do this for years, even when I was more skeptical of climate change than I am now. Years ago, I let her teach on the environment for a semester in our K-12 school. She had a major and positive impact on our students. I would have liked for her to continue, even though I do not agree with her perspective on everything she teaches.

Again, I understand that the producers of this documentary are filmmakers. It is standard procedure in the industry to exaggerate or add to the narrative of films on true stories to make them more interesting. Whether this is right or not is debatable, but it has become acceptable practice. That being said, documentaries should be on another level of devotion to accuracy. This kind of embellishment in a documentary reduces it to a much lower class of work called propaganda.

Because of certain things I have allowed to be taught in our schools, some have asked me if I purposely permit people to teach things in our churches and schools that I think are wrong. I do purposely let people of opposing views teach in our schools and speak in our churches, because I am deeply committed to the necessary freedom of debate in the pursuit of truth. I want our students committed to hearing all legitimate sides of an issue, learning to think and evaluate for themselves. I also want them to have respect for those who have different views and treat them with respect. They can do this if they have confidence in their ability to judge the information rightly.

I'm thankful we can have such disagreements in our family and yet remain close. I prayed for my children to be strong, independent thinkers, and to have their own conversion to Christ. I did not want them to believe anything just because I did, but to have their own faith in God and their own beliefs that they have established in their own quest for truth.

Okay, I overshot the runway on this! They are all far too strong and independent! Seriously, I'm very proud of each one, though it has sometimes been hard to watch them follow some of the courses they have chosen. Even so, I don't believe they will be strong enough for these times if they do not go through their own crises of faith and establish their own faith and relationship to God, and to the important issues of this world.

Truth requires freedom. Can anyone love because they are ordered to? In a warning about the end of this age, the Apostle Paul declares that those who are deceived are those who do not have "a love for the truth" (see II Thessalonians 2:10). That is much more than just having truth.

The Accuracy of the *Years* Project

Of course, I could not help but wonder that if the producers of *Years of Living Dangerously* were this loose with the facts about me and my relationship with Anna, how badly would they spin the rest of the story? My conclusion is that the spin was significant. I thought that the accounts in which I was personally involved were portrayed quite differently than what I witnessed. That being said, the documentary was actually not as bad as I had expected. It was still far from being accurate, but I was really expecting it to be much worse.

There were things that came out during the taping of our episode that I thought seriously challenged the basic premise of climate change. None of those were included. The story will ultimately be told by the editors, and nothing that seriously challenged their position on climate change made it through editing. That was disappointing, but not unexpected.

This was deceptive, but was it dishonest? I'm not sure. How could it be deceptive but not dishonest? I understand that you may think I'm being naïve and that the editors absolutely knew what they were doing. That could be true. However, I also witnessed some things that strongly implied that they really were not intentionally being dishonest. Understanding this could be as important as understanding anything about this issue.

After taping sessions for this documentary, I was constantly amazed by how those who were a part of it saw it so differently than I did. Often they heard the opposite of what I heard. A basic that we must understand about deception is that when you are so committed to seeing something, or so desperately want to see something, you will see it, and you will likely overlook anything that contradicts what you want to see.

I came to the conclusion that some who were involved in this project were not capable of seeing anything that did not fit their predetermined narrative. Of course, they would very likely say the same thing about me, and they could be right. However, I really was not a skeptic because I wanted to be. Throughout much of the time we worked on this project, I really wanted to see convincing proof of climate change. Even so, I could have been more biased than I realized.

We will discuss this in more depth later. Understanding why and how this happens could be basic to understanding much of the deception of our time.

Deception is Deceptive

One basic about deception we need to keep in mind is that when you are deceived, you do not know you are deceived or you would not be deceived. Those who are the most vulnerable to deception are those who think they have never been deceived, or are too smart for it to happen to them. Remember, Captain Smith was chosen as the skipper of the Titanic because he had never had an accident at sea. To never have experienced failure or deception can make you the most vulnerable. When you start to think you can't, you are likely in for one of the biggest failures of all.

Christians have also been just as prone to various kinds of deception throughout history. When dogma is esteemed above truth, strange things happen to people. It can happen to anyone when they seek to prove an already predetermined position. Believe it or not, like it or not, people do tend to see what they want to see. This can cause you to resist seeing a mountain of evidence that disproves your position, while embracing a molehill that supports it. This is happening within many of the sciences and movements, Christian and otherwise. Thankfully, there are some true scientists who are starting to raise their voices to expose this. Just as thankfully, there have been many great Christian leaders in history who have done the same for our faith.

I have no reason to accuse anyone who I worked with on this project of intentional deception, distortion, or dishonesty. Yet there was deception, distortion, and the portrayal of some things that I think were the opposite of what actually happened. We'll discuss some of these, but understanding how this happens can be as important as understanding this issue of climate change. And the same is being done with almost every major issue in these times.

My Deception

Through the experience of working on this documentary, I also came to realize how I had misjudged some people, and even some people groups. I had biases that caused me to misjudge them, and this too is deception.

Throughout the year, I grew in my appreciation and respect for those I worked with on this project. I did not grow in my respect for them just because it was the right thing to do, but because they earned it. They were respectful and respectable. The cynic might think this is a case of "the

Stockholm Syndrome" since I was such a lonely and embattled skeptic in this project, but I don't think so.

These were all extremely likeable people, and I enjoyed working with them. However, respect is more than merely liking someone. Liking them can help, but you can disrespect someone you like and like someone you disrespect. These were not only top professionals with an amazing devotion to excellence, but most seemed inquisitive, wanting to learn, and that is one thing I greatly respect. When the taping was over, I was surprised at the emails I received thanking me for not compromising my convictions. I believe these were sincere.

If we are sincere seekers of truth, to be shown where we are wrong or have a bias we didn't realize, is more than just a valuable thing, it is a great treasure. According to the Book of Proverbs, the wise "love reproof" (see Proverbs 12:1). I don't know if I'm wise enough yet to really love it, but I am thankful for it. If some of this happens to you through this narrative, I pray that you will embrace it. These reproofs are required if we are going to know the truth.

Some of the most influential people in my life were not people I liked or respected at first. I later recognized that I often felt this way about people who were different from me in some basic way. Had I not recognized this when I was young, I think my life would have been infinitely more shallow and fruitless. I did recognize it and intentionally began to seek out people who I knew were different so that I could learn from them. However, here I am, still guilty of biases against people in a whole profession. Intellectually I knew not to do this, but I was still doing it without realizing it. That's deception.

The Business of Life

One aspect that made me skeptical of climate change was the tendency of some proponents to attack business and business leaders. That is the same kind of deception I had fallen into and described above. For years, I have thought that one of the biggest deceptions on humanity is our tendency to judge people or people groups by their most extreme elements. That is bias, a form of bigotry.

Because I once owned an air charter service, most of my customers and many of my friends were top business leaders. Rogue CEO's and corporations that would scorch the earth for a profit do exist, but they are the extremes, and they are rare. Painting business and business leaders with such a broad brush is wrong. Most business leaders have children and grandchildren for whom they absolutely want to leave the world better, and they would be willing to make huge sacrifices to do so.

However, it must be even more difficult for business leaders to be open to climate change when they are so often attacked by those who espouse it. To their credit, there are many who surprisingly remain open to it, or even believe it, and want to be part of the solution in dealing with it. Whether you are a climate change skeptic or believer, this kind of noble spirit should be honored. It is a tragic and strategic mistake for the environmental movement not to build relationships with business owners. Instead they make them enemies by constantly taking shots at them.

There are also plenty of extreme and unnecessary attacks by conservatives on environmentalists. Some businesses have been behind this. Such polarization is common in causes because having an antagonist is one of the most effective ways to motivate your base, as well as to recruit. However, if we are to get to the truth of an issue, we must learn to tune out those who, in this way, muddy the waters of true debate. Those who have truth on their side should not need to resort to pressuring, bullying, intimidating, or manipulating. We can be fairly sure that those who use such tactics are trying to stand on a weak position and are, therefore, easily threatened by those who are not perceived as standing with them.

If man-made climate change is real, or it isn't, the climate of the heart of the people will ultimately determine the actions that are taken. We may completely convince someone that their actions are doing harm to the environment, but they won't change unless the underlying selfishness, greed, and/or insecurities are not dealt with.

For this reason, it is possible that this "most important issue of our time" could be a rare opportunity to make a real change in the climate of the heart. That will only come with understanding, and understanding can only come when we are willing to stand under someone else's place attempting to see from their perspective. Seeing a little of this magnanimity on one side of the issue can begin to open up those on the other side, but it will have a huge impact on those who are undecided.

Going into this project, I did not know many, and maybe not any, sincere attempts on either side of the climate change issue to understand the other side. It did surprise me when some of the producers working on the *Years* project made what I thought were sincere efforts to understand the basis of my skepticism and to accurately record it on tape. This gave me hope. I had decided that if these reasons were straightforwardly and honestly presented in the documentary, I would not have to write this book. But that is why I'm writing.

4

My Credentials

The powerful trailer to *The Years Of Living Dangerously* documentary begins with James Cameron asking if a patient had ninety-nine doctors agree on their condition, would they get another opinion? Obviously not. So if 99% of all scientists agree on climate change, why are we still debating it? My first question was, "Where did they get this number—99% of all scientists agreeing on climate change?" What I found by asking this was a revelation.

My first surprise was when no one seemed to know where this 99% number came from. The most common answer I got was, "Everyone knows this." That should always be a red flag! Others were a little more forthcoming saying that the actual number was 95%. A few even went as far as to say the actual number was probably 90%. Still, I could not find anyone who could tell me where these numbers came from.

Even if the percentage of scientists agreeing on this were true, it could have much more to say about how far science has fallen. To the true scientist, this would be cause for alarm, not trust. We'll discuss this more later. I know many scientists, including environmental and climate scientists. Except for those I met doing the *Years* project, I have not yet talked to one who was not at least skeptical about man-made climate change. You may think this is because of the conservative, Christian circles I generally move in. Perhaps. However, I have met these scientists on airplanes, at ball games, and other public places, and the same has held true.

Much more alarming was how, with the exception of those who had retired, I could not find a scientist who would go on record with their skepticism. This is because of the potential consequences they would suffer. For anyone who cares about truth, that kind of intimidation within a community, society, or profession should be one of the biggest alarms. In Christian circles, this would be considered cultic.

Therefore, having trouble finding where this figure of "99% of all scientists agree" came from, I went to the place where everyone goes if they want answers—Google. The only thing I could find was a remote poll done by the University of Illinois. You can make a poll say anything you want by the questions you ask. In this poll, thousands of scientists were sent two general questions, to which, in my opinion, it would have been difficult for anyone to answer "no." It seems that 90% of the scientists agreed with the foolishness of this poll and did not even bother to answer it. Of the 10% that did respond, only 5% of those were climate scientists.

I was a builder once, and I understand the principle that if your foundation is off, the higher you build, the further off plumb line you will be. The higher you go with a foundation that is not level, the greater the danger of collapse. Some of the foundations of climate change are tilted. It is hard to find a climate change proponent that will hear this, much less accept it, but the credibility of the climate change issue is cracking, and in many places collapsing.

This is in spite of the United Nations, the United States Government, and the other powers trying to shore it up. Many of those who recognize this eroding of the credibility of the argument blame it on the negative media. That is a ridiculous argument, since the overwhelming majority of media coverage of this is pro climate change. Maybe it has to do with the inability to hear challenges, which in itself reveals a serious flaw when it comes to any science

Statements like "99% of all scientists agree..." fly in the face of a basic premise of science which requires that we "challenge everything, doubt everything, never stop questioning..." To the thinking person, this looks more like pseudo science than real science.

In an interview before the Heartland Institute's 9th International Conference on Climate Change, Apollo Astronaut Walter Cunningham was a bit more brazen and was quoted in the report released by Craig Bannister on July 2, 2014. After studying the global warming/climate change issue for fourteen years, he said, "Climate alarmism is the biggest fraud in the field of science and the 97% consensus claim is nonsensical." He contended that not even a majority of scientists were convinced of climate change.

My Credentials

Astronaut Cunningham has impressive credentials for addressing this issue. Mine are not so much, but maybe more than you would think and maybe more than many of those today who are considered authorities on this topic.

Credentials are important. If you are to consider what I have to say on a subject, then you deserve to know the basis for my position. Degrees are a legitimate credential, if they are from a legitimate school. The more respect there is for a school, the more highly regarded that degree will be. The concept for having degrees from schools actually came from the Apostle Paul's letters of recommendation. Those letters would mean a lot coming from Paul—if you respected Paul.

I have a doctorate in what some consider the ultimate science, which I will explain later, and it is from a well-accredited school. However, the scope and arguments for and against climate change range far beyond science. They reach into politics, psychology, economics, morality, and ethics, as well as math and science. So I will address my credentials and perspectives on these fields as well.

I study science continually. I am not a professional doing it for my work, but I do it out of love for science and the knowledge I gain from it. I also do it out of a sense of responsibility to understand the important issues of our time. Even so, I admit that my studies are not the kind of systematic study that a professional scientist would do, and I am not presuming that. Even so, my credentials for understanding this issue may be more substantial than you might think.

I also have credentials for knowing and understanding weather and climate that may be the best one can have. I was a professional pilot who lived in weather. I almost daily crossed one or two weather systems and often flew into different climates. You cannot understand weather without understanding climate, and without understanding weather and climate you are not likely to live long as a pilot. I learned about weather and climate as if my life depended on it... because it did. So my credentials are that *I'm still here.*

My Filter

Regardless of credentials, we all have filters through which we process information. These can be biases, prejudices, disappointments, or bad experiences. Some of my prejudices and biases surfaced during the taping of this documentary, and I will be candid about them. First of all, I will address them because you deserve to know, and secondly, in case you might have the same ones, for they can be some of the biggest traps that keep us from the truth.

We can also have positive influences such as having someone we like on one side of the debate, as well as political or economic interests, etc. Having these filters does not necessarily mean that our beliefs are not true, but we should consider how they can color what we believe.

My Objective

I don't think I have a compelling motive for being on either side of the climate change debate, except for having a daughter that is deeply committed to it and all of my children take it very seriously. For their sakes, the sake of their children, and for all coming generations, I want to know the truth about this issue. I also want to know the truth because I think God gave us one of the most remarkable gifts of all in giving us this planet, and I cannot love or honor God without loving and honoring His gifts.

I agree that if climate change is real, man caused, and has potential consequences as bad as some are predicting, we must act quickly and resolutely. We must determine a workable strategy for stopping it as quickly as possible. If it is not real, or as extreme or damaging as some are claiming, then to react in such hysteria will almost certainly cause us to overreact and cause more damage than climate change. It is important that we not succumb to the pressures and understand who is behind the hysteria and why.

My Office Was The Sky

Again, a big part of my personal grid for being interested in and understanding climate change comes from being a pilot for most of my life, and a professional pilot for much of it. To become Airline Transport Rated, I was required to study weather and climate in a depth that some claimed was equal to getting a doctorate on the subject. I not only attained this rating, but I trained others for it, including some of our best military fighter pilots. This forced me to go deeper in my understanding of these subjects, but I had an even greater motive than this.

When I became a professional pilot in the 1970s, weather forecasting was so inaccurate that we would be surprised when a forecast was correct. Even though meteorology is still the butt of many jokes, it no longer deserves to be. It has improved in accuracy and dependability probably as much as any science over this period of time. I still fly my own plane and have stayed in touch with these impressive advancements in meteorology. I am extremely thankful for them every time I have to travel.

When I started flying professionally in the 1970s, it was common for pilots to face conditions that were not forecast. I determined that if I was going to live long in that job, I would need to know more about the weather than the forecasters. I set about to study everything I could get my hands on about the weather. I talked to every older, experienced pilot I came across to glean from their knowledge. There is a saying, "There are old pilots and bold pilots, but no old bold pilots." Most of the bold ones who did not get old were too bold with weather.

To fly an airplane would get you killed if you did not understand weather. Most crashes are caused by pilot error. Most pilot errors are caused by flying into weather conditions they are not prepared for, experienced enough to handle, or their aircraft is not equipped to handle. So, understanding weather and climate, and climate changes, is vital to pilots. Though I was initially motivated to understand this out of necessity, it became a passion. I started to love everything about weather. I have logged a lot of time flying, but I may have logged just as much time watching The Weather Channel, because I love learning about weather.

Every time I go into a weather station for a flight briefing, I try to learn something. Eventually I became good at forecasting. My goal was to never be surprised by any weather condition that I encountered on any flight. I got close to achieving this. I could pick up a forecast and quickly see any problems it had, correct them, and fairly accurately tell what it should be.

It was not uncommon to fly across two frontal systems in a single flight, or go from tropical temperatures to sub-zero, or vice versa. These changes can have major affects on the aircraft's performance. Because I flew jets, even on the hottest summer day in the tropics I would cruise at altitudes where the outside air temperature could be minus seventy degrees. Every flight was different, and every flight was an education.

The kind of education you get from actually doing something can be quite different from just reading books about it or studying it in school. There was a time when I was flying professionally when I didn't think I ever met a meteorologist or climatologist who knew as much as I did. To their credit, at least the meteorologists treated pilots as if we knew more than they did. They would humbly ask pilots for weather information because we were actually out there in the conditions. They still do so to this day, happily finding out any mistakes they made so they can do better in the future. I think this was a key to their remarkable advancements. They loved the truth more than their egos.

My respect for meteorologists has only grown with the passing of time. I know supercomputers have much to do with how accurate they have become, but you still have to feed accurate information into a computer to obtain the right results. What they have done is extremely impressive. However, it does not seem that climatologists have even come close to rising to the level of accuracy that meteorologists have accomplished. Why?

Granted, climate can be far more complex, and it deals with decades, centuries, or even longer. Even so, in general, it seems that climate science is where weather science was almost fifty years ago in accurate forecasting.

Whoever is advising President Obama on this subject is seemingly a climatologist and not a meteorologist. In a speech he gave in November 2013, he said that we would see record high temperatures in the coming winter. The opposite was the case as thousands of records for low temperatures were broken. In fact, that winter was the coldest since 1912.

When I have mentioned this to climatologists, the response was that other parts of the world did experience record highs. That is true, in some cases, but not overall. Weather is always seeking equilibrium, as this causes weather changes. If there is a record high in one place, then there will be a corresponding low somewhere else. However, overall the earth is in a period of cooling, not warming, which is measurable and has been well verified. This is why they changed the term "global warming" to "climate change."

Of course, the President is not a climatologist, but a politician. His speechwriters are politicians, not scientists. They may not have gotten the memo that we now call it "climate change" instead of "global warming." Even so, with his own obviously flawed understanding of what is happening with the climate, he is making climate change one of his major agendas. Why would anyone trust someone who has proven so inaccurate? If we cannot accurately forecast, then there is something fundamentally wrong with our fundamentals. Let's get them right before proposing what to do.

I say this as a sincere friend of climate science and meteorology, but this change from "global warming" to "climate change" has made the whole argument look silly to thinking people. This alone has generated a wave of skepticism in the whole premise of man-made climate change. I'm not necessarily saying this is fair, but it is true.

There was one climate model that did foresee the present cooling period, which projected that it would last ten to fifteen years and then the warming would begin again. This accurate climate forecast came from one who I think is as close to the highest ideals of a true scientist of anyone I've met, and he was a climate change skeptic at the time he began his research. The model that forecast this present cooling period with such accuracy did indicate, to his surprise, that man-made climate change is in fact real. We will cover this in more detail later.

That being said, most of the climate models that were driven by the global warming premise, and now climate change, have been far off the mark with what has actually unfolded. I have heard many explanations for this, such as the oceans absorbing more of the heat than they expected, ad infinitum. Again as a friend, these just make the whole premise start to sound silly. What would really help their credibility would be the ability to admit some mistakes and thereby learn from them.

Again, people tend to see what they are looking for. Climate science right now seems to have runaway prejudice toward proving climate change, which is alarming to a true scientist and others who just want the truth.

I now trust meteorologists many times more than I did in the 1970s, because they have earned my trust. Even so, when I pilot, I check out every forecast to examine it for possible flaws because, as good as they have gotten, they still miss at times. Based on their forecasts, climatologists still have a long way to go to earn my trust. Talking a good game is not the same as playing a good game—we need to see some accuracy.

My Science Degree

Continuing with my credentials, as stated I have a doctorate in what I consider the highest science of all—theology. I don't think there is a better way to understand the creation than by understanding the Creator. Theology also deals with how God and man have inter-reacted, as well as how mankind tends to act under different situations. Many of these actions and reactions are repeated in every generation, verifying the proverb that "Those who do not know history are doomed to repeat it." Believe it or not, we have been around this same mountain with the climate change debate many times.

History is quickly forgotten, and we could avoid many unnecessary problems by knowing history. For this reason, I have given many more hours a week to studying history than just about any other subject, except God. I have mostly studied church history, military history, and economic history, because these have had the greatest impact on the unfolding trends of history, but now science has taken its place as a major shaper of our time. For this reason, I've studied the growth of science, and it follows the same pattern as just about every other discipline. There is a remarkable parallel between church history and the history of science.

Some of the sciences are now falling into the same traps that Christianity fell into after the first century A.D. These traps led to over a thousand years of what historians call the

"Dark Ages." If these traps are not understood and avoided, science is headed for just such a time of darkness, and it will drag much of mankind with it, just like the church did.

Again, Christianity fell into this terrible darkness when political expediency caused dogma to be esteemed above truth. This led to the darkest times in human history. Jesus, the apostles, and the early church fathers all warned that this would happen, but few heeded their warnings. After over a thousand years of this terrible darkness, an awakening began. Now after six hundred years of reformation and the recovery of truth, the church is still digging its way out of the mire it had fallen into. It would be great if the church's mistakes could be used to keep science from making the same ones.

One of my chief alarms about the climate change hysteria is that it contains all of the elements that took the church so far off course. This led to the crushing perversion of truth. It does seem that the same kind of political agendas are threatening to do the same to science with climate change being the point of the spear. If climate change is real, this is even more of a potential tragedy.

Christianity, in its pure form, is true even though evil or misled people have often perverted it, used it for their own gain, or used it for the control of or oppression of others. For this reason, we must also consider that there may be truth to the premise of climate change even if it is seemingly now being hijacked for political agendas.

My Biggest Filter

When I was discharged from the Navy in 1970, I was not a Christian and never expected to become one. I did not become one because I was intellectually persuaded by the truth of Christianity, but because of a supernatural conversion experience. It was the kind of conversion the Apostle Paul had in Scripture. I was knocked off of my high horse and instantly shown how blind I was, but I was also shown how real God is *and* how deeply He cares about the affairs of this world. From that day, I have not doubted that God is real and who He is. I don't even know if I could doubt, because the experience was so powerful.

I consider my supernatural conversion to be the grace of God because I was so hardhearted or hardheaded, or both. I was not even seeking to know God, though I did make a casual prayer one day that if there was a God, I would like to know Him. I also made a commitment that if He would reveal Himself to me, then I would try to spend the rest of my life serving Him. The prayer was sincere, at the moment anyway, but I never expected it to be answered. This is a most dangerous prayer, and I do not recommend praying it unless you mean it. Of those I know who have prayed it, I do not know of one who did not get it answered.

I understand that most have not had this kind of experience, so I don't expect them to believe the way that I do. I try to keep in mind that I was once not a follower of God and was on a trajectory with my life to be an evil, selfish person. I do not consider myself better than anyone else now. I am just one who has received grace, and I remain far more selfish than I should be with all of the grace I have received.

That being said, those who believe in God tend to be those who want to, and those who don't believe are those who don't want to. This has nothing to do with whether God is real or not, but with people's preferences. Knowing how real He is indicates to me that He has given us remarkable freedom. He only wants followers who want to follow Him, because He could easily prove how real He is anytime He wanted.

Having been a believer for over forty years, I know that those who do not want to believe in God will likely reject a mountain of evidence that supports His existence and embrace a molehill that supports what they want to believe. He allows this, now. There is a time coming when all will know how real He is, but now He is sifting the hearts of men.

Likewise, a Christian who is committed to a certain dogma can reject a mountain of evidence that counters it and embrace a molehill that supports it. We humans have a problem with objectivity, but if we understand and accept this, we can navigate through it to the truth.

I know many who probably know God much better than I do and have more faith than me. Even so, God is the chief fascination in my life, and His creation is next. This begins with what Scripture calls "the new creation." As wonderful and perpetually fascinating as the physical creation is, the "new creation" is many times more so.

The "new creation" is comprised of those who have accepted the atonement that God has provided so that we can be reconciled to Him through the cross, and then join with Him reconciling and restoring mankind and the earth. The biblical prophets, who prophesied so much that has already come true and have been thereby proven accurate, predicted this restoration of the earth as a cornerstone to their prophecies. This is a key to understanding true Christianity—those who are restored must become restorers.

This "new creation" is being made into the ultimate society that will be used to restore the earth to the paradise it was originally created to be. This includes restoring mankind to the place we were created to have. We see this in such places as Isaiah 11 where we are even promised that the lion will lie down with lambs and children will be able to play with cobras. The foundation of this restoration is already being laid, and all of creation will be fully restored.

So why should we worry so much about the environment now? In the most famous of all Scripture verses, John 3:16, we are told that God so loved the world that He gave His own Son for its redemption. God loves "the world" that much, not just mankind. He loves all of His creatures, even the ugly, slimy, and creepy ones I may not think too much of. So if we love Him, we will love and take care of what He loves.

It has been estimated that between one-third and one-half of the biblical teachings on righteousness have to do with stewardship. The first responsibility that God gave us was to be stewards over the earth. We will not be fully restored until this has been recovered.

Man has been redeemed by the atonement sacrifice of Jesus and must be reconciled to God and restored before we can be the stewards we are called to be. For this reason, I am in full agreement that the preaching of the gospel must be first, but there is more to preparing the way for the Lord than sharing the gospel. In Isaiah 40, we are told that to prepare the way for the Lord, we must build a highway. That highway is the great work of our time. This issue can help us understand this great work.

Now that you have a basic understanding of my perspective, you can judge how much of what I am sharing may have been colored by it. Let's now go back to the issue of climate change.

5

To Believe or Not to Believe in Climate Change

Before continuing, let us do a little self-evaluation. Consider the categories below and note which one you think best describes your present position on man-made climate change.

Total Believer—no doubt that climate change is real, and human beings are causing it.

Believer—have not had the chance to examine the science or the arguments in depth, but I believe that it is true.

Open—either have listened to the arguments on both sides and have not been persuaded by either, or have not had or taken the time to examine this issue enough to be persuaded by either side.

Skeptic—have concluded that there are more reasons to doubt than to believe in man-made climate change, but still remain open to there being something to it

Denier—completely convinced this is a major ruse, a farce, and there is no truth to it whatsoever.

There can be legitimate reasons for an intelligent, thinking person to be in any one of these categories. There are also degrees to each of these categories, even the extremes of total believer or total denier. For example, there are people who are believers who have done substantial research on the subject and those who haven't. Likewise, there are skeptics and deniers who have done substantial research and those who have not.

I rated myself a skeptic when I started work on the documentary, thinking I was about 60% skeptical and 40% open. I am still a skeptic, though I may have moved a little bit more toward "open." I'm sure I appear stubborn to many who have tried to persuade me one way or the other, especially those who worked with me on the *Years* project. However, for important issues I think it is right to require substantial evidence. I'm really not trying to take a position to please or annoy anyone. I would love to settle the issue and move on. I just have not seen convincing proof yet. If it is out there, I would love to find it, regardless of which way it pushed me.

The best of all the studies I've seen, which I think was done by one of the finest true scientists of our time, gives some convincing evidence of climate change being real and caused by man. However, this study also found that the change of climate has been quite small—a little over a half degree over the last half-century. This is certainly not enough to panic over, but it is enough to get our attention.

If this is caused by the increased CO_2 in the atmosphere, man adds about 3½% of the CO_2 put in the atmosphere, and nature does the rest—96½%. Remove man's contribution and there probably would be no change at all, or it might be on the decreasing side. Thinking like a true scientist, the leader of this research team said that the first thing we needed to determine was whether or not this slight increase was having a negative affect. To me, that seemed like the kind of reason and sanity rarely heard on either side of this argument. We will get into this more later.

Some of the most vehement proponents of climate change have admitted that the evidence is strong that the real temperature change has been about sixth-tenths of one degree over the last half-century. The studies that indicate this are solid, but not infallible. Nature contributes 96½% of the CO_2 that is being put into the atmosphere from volcanoes, forest fires, and many other sources. A main natural contributor is cattle passing gas because of the way they process their food. My question is, why don't we make the cows stop farting and leave us alone?

The Cure Can Be Worse Than the Disease

There are actually studies being done about how we might reduce the gas in cows, but this raises some other questions. Once we can calm down, remove the rhetoric, and get to what is actually happening, we must be careful in proposing solutions, if solutions are even needed. After all, CO2 is plant food. That is why it is called a "greenhouse gas," because they pump it into greenhouses to cause the plants to grow faster.

The vegetation on the earth loves the extra CO2 it is getting. Because plants are near the beginning of the food chain, most other creatures are probably loving it too. How do we know that this is not a good thing? It is encouraging that some of the most reputable scientists on the planet are now having the courage to ask this question.

There are many questions we should be asking before we start proposing remedies, which may or may not be helpful. Some remedies, made in haste and driven by panic, have had dire consequences in the past. Probably everyone in the South knows about kudzu (and it is creeping north). Plants and animals that have been introduced to regions they are not native to have often become much bigger problems than the ones they were introduced to solve.

Many think this is people playing God, but I don't agree. We are not playing God by seeking to control the environment, because God gave us that commission. However when this commission was given, mankind walked with God, and He expected us to do it together with Him. Without God's wisdom, we could make problems much worse, and often have, even with the best of intentions and the best science available at the time.

Sound decisions are rarely made under panic. I have had co-pilots become a bigger problem when they panicked than the actual emergency we were facing. I have learned not to trust those who are driven by fear, are reactionary, or prone to panic or hysteria.

Processing Information

We have briefly addressed filters, but we need to dig down into this a bit more. I make a living through writing and public speaking. It is rewarding to hear from people who were helped by something I said or wrote. It is also alarming how virtually every time I speak someone will tell me afterward they are glad that I said something that I know I did not say. Often they will say I said something I do not even believe, or is the opposite of what I believe. It is more rare for people to do this when reading something I wrote, but it happens sometimes there too. Again, many people will only hear what they want to hear. Jesus warned us to "be careful *how* you hear" (see Mark 4:24). That is still a valid warning.

Again, we all have filters through which we perceive the world. They often color and distort what we are seeing. If you think you don't have filters, you are probably one of the most deceived of all. To be true to ourselves and to discern truth, we need to understand our own filters.

The Conservative Filter

Let's take a moment to try and understand the mind of a political conservative. I think I can do this, because I am one. However, remember that in order to understand, we have to stand under their position to see from their perspective. To understand something does not mean you agree with it, but understanding can help.

Conservatives believe that liberals know very well that they are not likely to win a national election without a crisis. This is actually based on writings and policy memos from liberals and history. Some have even said that if there is not a crisis, invent one. Therefore, conservatives have a knee-jerk reaction to any crisis that seems to fit the liberal agenda.

As early as the 1930s, when the Communist Party in the U.S. started calling themselves "progressives" because of the increasing unpopularity of Stalin, one of their stated strategies was to use "the ecology movement" to keep the youth radicalized. Conservatives are educated about things like this, and they tend to look at a lot of issues through this perspective.

The man-made climate change crisis seems too much like this continual drumbeat of invented crises, especially using the environmental movement.

Most who are old enough remember that in the 1960s and 70s the mantra was global cooling. The fear was that we were causing another ice age by the burning of fossil fuels. So the whole global warming issue sounded ridiculous to those old enough to remember this. Can you really blame them? It just looks like science cannot get its story about crises straight. Then, when the global warming crisis name was changed to "climate change" it looked even more foolish. This is not to say that it is, but it appears this way.

The key words here are "on the surface." Most people do not have the time or expertise to do deep research. However, they have been fooled before, and this just seems all too familiar. Believe it or not, our parents warned us in the 1960s and 70s that this was a ruse, and we did not believe them. As much as we thought we knew better than they did, they were right. For this reason, it is going to take far more substance than before to be convinced of this.

Also, most of those who lived through the 1960s and 70s, who are now in their 60s and 70s, were educated on Saul Alinsky's, *Rules For Radicals*. Though we may have enjoyed using these tactics back then, now we recognize them and will consider those who use them as enemies of truth and democracy. They can work for short-term results but almost always ultimately backfire. Those who use them will be considered evil deceivers because only those who do not have the truth or reason on their side need to use them.

As far as motives, as I have said, I felt that everyone I worked with on this project sincerely believed that climate change is real, man caused, and likely is the greatest crisis of our time. That does not mean that there is not an agenda further up the line. You cannot survive as a pastor for as long as I have without being able to spot people with agendas. I felt that all of the people I worked with on *Years* were sincere. However, being sincere is not the same as being right.

I also felt, until the last day of taping, that pressure was put on me emotionally to convert. Emotionally this was difficult. It is hard to be possibly the only skeptic of something that everyone else you are working with not only sees differently, but really thinks is the worst crisis threatening the earth. Trust me, I wanted to believe in man-made climate change many times. Then, at times, the more emotional and political pressure that I felt, the more I wanted to bow up and resist. That is not good for objectivity either, and I tried not to become too jaded through the process.

However, I came close to becoming an absolute man-made climate change denier, thinking the whole thing is the greatest ruse of our time. I did not want to end up there, but I felt that this is where the evidence led. Then, in a day, I was finally presented with evidence that was not only objective science, but with reason and wisdom that was like seeing blue sky for the first time in a long time.

For this reason, regardless of which of the above five categories you are in, I am not trying to move you to a new category. The studies and links to studies I will provide on the website may do this, but what I am trying to do is bring some clarity and understanding to those of any position, which can hopefully lead to the truth and then proper action. Even if the science exists that could absolutely prove any of these positions, it will likely be rejected if it is not presented in the right way, properly navigating the minefields left by other issues that proved not to be true.

That being said about the conservative filter, conservatives and environmentalists should be allies, not enemies. The word *conservation* comes from *conservative*. With the message presented in a better way, conservatives can become open, and if convinced, they will be some of the most effective advocates for protecting the earth.

All Truth?

Just a note here about those who make statements like, "All true scientists..." Regardless of their position, those who make such statements are simply not telling the truth. This is a primary reason why the argument for man-made climate change has been losing credibility. Only when true science has been abandoned are such statements possible.

Again, let us not forget that every cause has immature, uneducated, or even unstable people who attach themselves to it. They can and will make foolish statements like this, but they should not be a basis for throwing the whole argument out. It is only when the leading proponents in a field make statements like this that something has gone seriously awry, and we should doubt their position.

We must also consider that even the best and brightest can exaggerate or say stupid things in the heat of a moment. When I was recently introduced to a man who is "one of the top climate scientists in the world," I asked him what he thought about the artic ice cap growing 40% last year. He said it was not true. Yet it is true and has been confirmed by both NASA and the European Space Agency photos. I was amazed that he was completely ignorant of this major finding, and I probably showed my astonishment. He shot back saying the fact was that the ice cap had shrunk by 80%. He seemed to immediately realize how stupid that statement was, and I did not know how to extricate him gracefully. I think I said something like he should read more, but that was equally as stupid and disrespectful. I don't think it is right to judge a person on one conversation, especially one that got as awkward as this one did.

We should not judge someone's entire work or perspective by such aberrations. Maybe we should all try live by the principle, "Let the one that has never made a stupid statement cast the first stone." Then we could all give some grace and also receive it. That would lead to a lot more understanding. When one refuses to admit their mistakes that are clearly revealed, we have a basic integrity issue.

Responsible stewardship is neither a liberal nor a conservative idea. It is not a religious or a political idea. Responsible stewardship of the land is a God idea.

- Dr. Roger L. DeHaan, *Creation Care: The Truth About "Living Green" and Healing Our Planet*

6

A Year of Living Dangerously

This is my account of some highlights of working on *The Years Of Living Dangerously* project itself, and what I thought were the important revelations that came from it.

Apalachicola

Apalachicola Bay is where a large percentage of oysters are harvested that supply seafood restaurants in the southeast. Being an oyster lover, it got my attention when I was asked if I could bring Anna Jane with me and spend a couple of days there examining how climate change was impacting the oysters.

Oysters are also an important part of the eco system. The environment was created with many filters and self-cleaning systems, and oysters are one for the oceans. Each oyster filters about one gallon of water per hour. Therefore, when oysters are depleted, the impact of pollution can be multiplied.

On this visit to Apalachicola, I was told that we would spend a day dialoging with Katharine Hayhoe, a top climatologist as well as an evangelical Christian married to an evangelical pastor. I thought it was a great opportunity so I cleared my schedule, and Anna and I took off in my little plane.

Oysters live in salt water, but near the mouths of rivers and streams because they need a certain amount of fresh water to lower the salinity in typical salt water in order to breed. The salinity in the Apalachicola Bay had risen to the point where they were not breeding as much, and the oyster population was decreasing. When we were there, we were told that the oysters were about two-thirds below the normal population.

Katharine is a very likable person. Her book, *A Climate For Change*, is causing some Christians to embrace climate change or at least be more open to it. I thought this could be the day for me to finally be convinced, and to be honest, I was excited about it.

Katharine began by stating rather emphatically that the destruction of the oysters was caused by climate change melting the ice caps, raising the sea level so that more of the salty Gulf water was pouring into the bay, thereby destroying the oyster population.

I was surprised by what I thought was a very unscientific approach to this, when we had not yet talked with anyone else there. I challenged this by stating that I have been going to the Gulf Coast every summer for thirty-six years and had not noticed any rise in the water levels. We also have a place on the North Carolina coast that we have been going to for eight years, and the talk there was about how the beaches are getting wider due to the falling water levels.

One of my friends on the North Carolina coast is a world-class sport fisherman who is widely known. He spends more time on the water than anyone I know and fishes all over the hemisphere. When I asked him about rising sea levels, he also said that it was the opposite. He expressed his alarm at how the sea levels are falling.

When I tried to bring this up to Katharine, the answers I got were that there was much data to prove that the sea levels are rising. Even so, with all of the recent revelations and scandals about the cooking of the numbers in many of the studies used by climate change advocates, I was far more prone to believe my own observations or the observations of those who make their living on the sea.

This was not a promising start to the day, but still if there was any truth to climate change, I was hoping that something would be convincing. When I thought Katharine's answers to my questions were superficial, and it began to feel like she was a professor lecturing a student, I tried to explain that I had more background on the science than she may have known, hoping she would raise the level of discussion. It did not work, even though I could tell she was trying not to come across like a lecturer. I could handle that, but it was disappointing not to hear anything that was convincing. In fact, some of her explanations were such a stretch that I felt even more concerned about climate science and more skeptical about climate change than when the day began.

Katharine Hayhoe has a growing reputation as a climate scientist and was just named among the one hundred most influential people in the world. She has paid a price for her stand on climate change, and I appreciate anyone standing with courage for what they believe. It just may not have been one of her better days, or one of mine, but I just could not make a connection with her explanations.

The highlight of the day was going out into the bay with father and son oystermen. I was tired of talking about the subject of climate change, but one of the directors told me that Arnold Schwarzenegger, one of the producers of the *Years* project, had insisted on "the cool factor." Arnold was right. This was one of the coolest things we did. These oystermen were such compelling characters that a show with them could rival *Duck Dynasty*. This was rich entertainment. They were absolute believers that climate change was destroying their oysters, and their explanations of how this was happening did not make a lot of sense to me, but it was great fun listening to them.

It got my attention that the oysterman who had the cameramen in his boat did not believe in climate change, but he did not get interviewed. In fact, I never saw anyone get interviewed who was a climate change skeptic, except myself. However, these are filmmakers, and "the cool factor" of the father and son team was great for entertainment.

The next day a eureka moment came that I thought clearly and overwhelmingly identified what was happening to the oysters in Apalachicola Bay. Anna and I were asked to interview four oystermen, each of whom had been making their living on the bay for over thirty years. I only had two questions for them: "What did they think was causing the oyster depletion? What did they think could be done about it?" Their answers immediately explained causes that had nothing to do with climate change.

The first oysterman said he believed the crisis was the result of a channel that the Corp of Engineers cut into the bay to let bigger ships through. This had been done decades before, but when it was no longer needed as a passage, the locks were not maintained, letting in much more water from the Gulf, changing the salinity of the bay. I was stunned. That alone could have been the cause of the oyster depletion.

The second oysterman agreed with the first, but said that he also studied the river sources into the bay. These originated above Atlanta, and Atlanta was using twice as much fresh water as it had just ten years before. Therefore, only about half of the fresh water was coming into the bay. This alone could have caused the problem too, but these two factors together certainly were having an impact.

The next oysterman said that when the BP oil spill hit, all of the oystermen on the Gulf of Mexico had been invited to come harvest the oysters in Apalachicola Bay before the oil killed them. They had fished the bay out. That alone could be the reason why the population was now only about a third of what it had been.

The fourth oysterman added that the drought in Georgia was a major factor as well. There had been a severe drought in eastern Georgia that was certainly a contributing factor to less fresh water coming down the rivers. So, in the *Years* episode, this drought was made to be *the* factor for the oyster crisis, and this drought was caused by climate change, yet none of the other factors were even mentioned.

When I saw this episode in *Years*, I was stunned by that level of spin. This was so disappointing that it became extremely challenging for me to believe any of the other stories in *Years*.

Even so, these are filmmakers. It is standard procedure for Hollywood to change, embellish, add to, or take away from true stories they are using to make them more interesting. In recent times, this has become standard procedure to fit in their political spin. I went into this project knowing and expecting it. I was still deeply disappointed to see it so blatant.

Ian Somerhalder narrated this part of the episode, but he was not there with us for the taping. He was likely just reading a script and had no idea that it was so far from what actually unfolded. I talked to the editor before I viewed the episode, and she was resolute that she had portrayed this accurately and that the drought was the cause of this catastrophe. That is when I started believing that some people have had a Jedi mind trick done on them and cannot see what is right in front of their eyes if it does not fit their predetermined narrative.

Has the long accepted practice of bending the facts to make films say what you want them to say caused these people to become so jaded that they cannot even recognize actual facts anymore? I really think this editor saw all that we taped and locked onto what could make this a climate change story—the drought, the molehill in the story, and missed the mountain of evidence that refuted it.

My daughter, Anna, is a stickler for facts and accuracy. She was with me through the whole thing. When I asked her about what was killing the oysters, she too said that it was the drought, which was caused by climate change. It was like she really had not seen or heard anything that did not fit this narrative. Jedi mind trick?

Similarly, I know many Christians can often have pet doctrines or other dogma, and they cannot see other Scriptures that counter their beliefs. I know some like this who are absolutely brilliant and deeply committed to the truth as they see it, but they cannot see the truth that conflicts with their bias. I have been guilty enough and am always looking for it in myself. I likely still have my own blind spots, but this level of distortion was troubling.

Politics in America is now so polarized that it seems almost impossible for the media to see or cover anything that does not fit their narrative or agenda. This can happen with the liberal or conservative media. I have always considered this dishonesty, but since working on this documentary, I have begun to see that at least some of it may not be dishonesty as much as blindness. This blindness is caused by bias. Those who are blinded in this way do not know it, because if you knew you were deceived, then you would not be deceived.

Droughts and Climate Change

Droughts are used in *Years* as evidence of climate change, but are they really? There have been droughts since the beginning of recorded history, long before we even knew there was such a thing as fossil fuels to burn. Why are all droughts suddenly man-made and caused by climate change? When I asked this question, I was told that climate change is making them worse. Really? The drought in Georgia that was supposedly the cause of the oyster disaster ended right after we did the taping there. Does that mean that climate change has now gone away? You can't have it both ways.

Because this one crisis, which was promoted as evidence of devastation caused by climate change, was not caused by climate change, it still does not disprove climate change. However, this is a good example of how the climate change mania has colored many people's minds so that they cannot see or even consider anything else. In this case, it caused them to miss the real causes, thereby being unable to do something about them. At least three of the factors hurting the oysters were man-made and preventable.

How many more environmental crises are not being understood and dealt with properly because the climate change mania is causing environmentalists to overlook other devastating factors that are destroying the environment? Things like mercury poisoning is hardly on anyone's radar scope anymore. Even the environmentalists who see this cannot speak out about it, because if you touch climate change, you will lose your grants and maybe your livelihood. That kind of intimidation is a major source of distortion and deception. It could be allowing much more damage to the planet than real man-made climate change is even capable of doing.

Again, I am not accusing anyone on the *Years* project of dishonesty, which I would do if I thought it was the case. I understand some may think I am just being naïve, and this may be true, but I am sure that the spin and distortion on this project was great, regardless of the motives. Those who were there and stand on the other side of this debate may read this and think I am the one doing the spinning, and that they really did not see it that way at all. I believe them. I think some are not capable of seeing or hearing anything that does not fit the climate change narrative. This is distorting what they see or blinding them from seeing the obvious, but that is not the same as dishonesty.

Now that is my subjective take on this. I realize very well that evidence at least points to someone up the food chain having an agenda. The whole time I was also looking for evidence that man-made climate change was real, I was looking for the "smoking gun"—who and why anyone would do this. I did find some interesting connections.

The U.S. Government declared Apalachicola Bay a disaster area just a few days after we left there. Their reasons for declaring it a disaster area were the factors shared with us by the four oystermen. There was no mention of climate change. In spite of the seemingly overwhelming evidence to the contrary, there are still honest people in government.

7

Ian Somerhalder
and Congressman Bob Inglis

The producers of *Years* wanted Anna and I to visit the home of former Republican Congressman Bob Inglis for some discussions. These were to be moderated by Ian Somerhalder, an actor, presently playing Damon in *The Vampire Dairies*.

Bob was from possibly the most conservative district in the South and maybe the nation. He had also become a believer in climate change and felt this had cost him his reelection. This sounded interesting, but I was not too excited about having an actor be the moderator. What could an actor really know about climate change? I stand corrected on this one too.

Ian quickly won me over as a man of uncommon depth and insight. Even more impressively, he had an ability to really listen, even to views that were not in agreement with his position on climate change. He was also quite likeable and shared one of my chief loves—a love for animals.

Bob Inglis is a nice man, a good Christian with a great family. He was still hurting from having lost the last election, and hurting people are not always themselves. It sounded like the Republican Party had quit supporting him because he was making climate change an issue. In listening to him, I think it was more likely that he was making climate change a main issue when the country was going through an economic meltdown—it was just bad timing and bad politics. Even so, I was looking forward to hearing the reason for his revelation about climate change. It must have been something really significant for him to make it an issue when and where he did.

I was surprised when Bob said that what made him believe in climate change was the compassion he felt for some people who were supposedly being hurt by it. Please don't get me wrong. In my profession, compassion is the basis for just about everything we do, so I appreciate compassion. I think Bob would make a great pastor, probably a much better one than I, but this is an issue of science. Our conclusions must be based on science, not compassion.

I hurt for those oystermen in Apalachicola, but in order to help them, we need to find the real cause of their suffering, which had nothing to do with climate change. The climate change narrative had everyone so distracted that no one was doing what could help them. I think this is happening far more than we realize. Compassion that helps people must be based on truth.

Then Bob questioned why I would go to the Internet and read both sides of the climate change debate! I admit to being shocked by this question probably more than anything I experienced that year. At first I thought he was joking. He was not. I was even more surprised that it made it through the cut and into the documentary, which I was thankful for.

How could I ever discern the truth if I did not listen to both sides of a debate? One of the main reasons I became a skeptic was because climate change believers seemed incapable of listening to challenges to their position. Remember, true science doubts everything, examines everything, and challenges everything.

Do I do this with my Christian faith? Yes. I have studied every major religion in some depth, as well as many of the major denominations within Christianity. I have studied other worldviews with considerable depth. This has not undermined my faith, but rather strengthened it. It has also fortified my belief that all people should be treated with dignity and respect regardless of their beliefs, with the exception of those whose mentality is so perverted that they could think it is right to kill innocent and defenseless people who disagree with them.

I also do not think anyone can be coerced into believing something and have the conversion be real. That is why God gave man freedom and put a tree in the garden that they were forbidden to eat from. He then left them alone so they could disobey Him if they chose to. There could be no true obedience without the freedom to disobey. They chose poorly, but God has never taken back our freedom to choose. Instead we are told, **"Where the Spirit of the Lord is, there is liberty" (see II Corinthians 3:17).**

Ian Somerhalder was refreshingly open to hearing my concerns about climate change. Until meeting him, I did not think anyone was really listening to my objections or questions, much less considering them. I could tell they were thinking of their comebacks rather than listening to me. I was going to see the project through because I was committed to it, but it was not encouraging until Ian gave me hope that there might be some true and meaningful dialog; answers and not lectures.

Not that I did not appreciate the lectures. They were opportunities to learn something, but they did not answer my questions. Ian's questions about my questions were not just rebuttals, but were deep, refreshingly insightful, and sincere. When I made a reasonable point, he would acknowledge it.

Meeting Ian was very encouraging. My respect for him grew the more we worked together.

Getting to know Ian convicted me of some of my stereotyping of actors and actresses. Of course, I appreciate them for the talent they have in their profession, but it seemed superficial to me when they endorsed certain causes or political candidates. How does being an actor or actress qualify them to endorse these things?

Actually, it is the same basis by which I have authority to write this book on climate change and expect anyone to read it. I have spent most of my life trying not to judge people based on externals, and here I was doing it with actors and actresses, even after one of my favorite Presidents, Reagan, had been an actor.

If you saw the first episode of *Years*, I don't know how you cannot respect the work that Harrison Ford did in Indonesia. Regardless of what you think of his position on climate change, he used his platform to courageously confront one of the great tragedies of our generation—the destruction of the rain forests. That being said, this does not mean all actors and actresses who endorse causes or people know what they are talking about. However, some may know more than we expect them to. I appreciate anyone who gets engaged in the important issues of our times, even if I disagree with them.

Ian came to our church and sat through one of my sermons. Afterward, he asked some questions that revealed his ability to listen on a level that is rare. He was open and insightful. As we taped sessions in my home and then in my office into the evening, I was impressed with his knowledge, but also his desire to learn more. He seemed to really want to understand my objections and consider them, not just refute them. What would happen to the trust people have for Christians if we were more like that?

As I said, my education working on this project was about much more than climate. I repeat, we cannot really understand others if we don't stand under their position to try to see as they do. Yet I had unfairly judged a whole profession. As a preacher who knows that the One I serve does not have a high opinion of hypocrites, I am always thankful for this kind of correction.

Martin Luther King, Jr.'s dream that no one would be judged by the color of their skin but by the content of their character came from the Apostle Paul. He wrote in II Corinthians 5:16 that we should only know people after the Spirit, not the flesh or externals. That should also carry over into categorizing people after their professions and where they may be from. We now call this stereotyping, and it leads to much evil.

I have been teaching for thirty years now that racism is one of the greatest evils of the human heart and the most destructive. It is one of the ultimate evils because it is built on two of the most destructive evils: pride and/or fear. It is at the root of most wars. It is a profoundly un-Christian characteristic. Deliverance from racism is one of the surest signs of true Christian maturity. Our God so loves diversity that He even makes every snowflake, as well as every leaf on every tree and every one of us, different. Therefore, true Christian maturity is to love and appreciate uniqueness. It is the ability to see beyond the superficial and to know others by their hearts.

Because the Scriptures repeat that the Lord will resist the proud, but give His grace to the humble (see James 4:6), what could be a more base form of pride than racism that is pride in the flesh? All forms of bigotry are a revelation that our minds have not yet been renewed to see from God's perspective.

My own professional bigotry was revealed. Then, when I watched the first episode of *Years* and marveled at what Harrison Ford did in Indonesia, I had to ask, where were the Christians? Why haven't we already been there confronting that terrible tragedy? We are supposed to be the most resolute freedom fighters taking up the cause of the poor and oppressed. If we call ourselves "prolife," how can we not be for all life?

This was the foundation for an important revelation that is one of the most profound I have had in a long time. I am still a climate change skeptic. I am not so slow to realize the political agenda that was behind the making of this documentary and how its release perfectly coincided with the Obama Administration's thrust on using climate change as a major political initiative. A person would be blind not to connect the dots to other globalist initiatives. However, in the midst of all of that, there are some who are fighting a battle that is dear to God's heart and is well established in the Scriptures. So we don't get too far off the course here, I will save that teaching for the end.

8

The Boston Massacre

After a long day of taping dialog between Ian, my daughter Anna, and myself, we had a few minutes left before the camera crew had to pack up and rush to the airport to catch their flight. In that last few minutes, Ian produced a number of graphs and studies, such as the "hockey stick graph." He then asked me how, with such overwhelming evidence, I could doubt all of this proof about climate change. Because the crew had to shut down, pack up, and run, I only had time to say there are other studies that have come to other conclusions.

I felt ambushed. This was a cheap shot like I had not seen from the producers before. I expressed to them how unfair that last session was. To my surprise, they agreed.

I had expected that if I did not convert to being a climate change believer then I would be presented as the caricature of the stubborn, white, Southern, conservative evangelical. I felt that the last session was their attempt to do just that. I also knew I had a recourse. I know the number of viewers of some of our MorningStar TV videos had at times eclipsed those of all of the news networks combined. All along I knew that if I felt they distorted anything, I would be able to answer it. But I was grieved. Even though at that point I felt the argument for man-made climate change was shakier than ever, I had gained a lot of respect for those doing this project. I felt they were sincere, but just misled. However, now that respect was shaken.

I proposed that the only fair way to present their graphs and studies was to give time to those who had done the same studies but come to different conclusions. I suggested taping the discourse between real scientists. They not only agreed to this, but liked the idea. They would try to work out a time and place to do this and asked me to find one or two climate scientists who were skeptics of climate change that would agree to this.

My disappointment over that last session still stung, but I went right to work looking for such climate scientists. There was no shortage. However, the ones who were not fearful of losing their job for expressing their skepticism tended to be angry or very condescending in their attitude toward any scientist who still believed in climate change. This was understandable for the abuse they had endured for their stand, but I was hoping for an open, honest, civil dialog that would be understandable to viewers from both sides. I was still hoping for convincing evidence of one side or the other. Until this search for a scientist, I did not realize just how divided and wounded much of the scientific community is because of this issue.

Then there is a problem shared by both sides of the debate: finding a top climate scientist who was articulate and able to express themselves well on camera. Some were articulate, but on a level only other scientists could understand, and not the average person.

Finally, one of the producers called and said he did not think the scientist dialog would work. However, they had one of the most respected and brilliant physicists and mathematicians who was listed as one of the one hundred most influential people in the world. They wanted me to present all of my objections and he would answer them.

Of course, that sounded like the biggest ambush of all to me. My trust in them at this point was almost as low as my belief in climate change. I may understand the science, but I am not a professional scientist. For me to go toe-to-toe with one of the best scientists in the world would certainly be a slaughter. When they said they wanted to do the taping in Boston, I immediately thought this would be another Boston Massacre.

So I agreed to do it. How could I resist? I follow the Lamb of God who went willingly to His execution.

A Good Day to Die

It was a stunningly beautiful day in Boston and turned out to be the day that the Boston Red Sox won the World Series. The setting was a great room overlooking the Boston Harbor. Anna had flown in, as well as Ian Somerhalder, who had canceled a day of taping *Vampire Diaries* so he could join us. Professor Richard Muller from the University of California at Berkeley was the executioner.

I met the professor, and we shared some small talk over coffee. I wanted to ask him some things about quantum physics. He wanted to talk about God! "I pray every day," he said. "Really. Who do you pray to?" I asked. "I don't know," he replied. "What do you pray?" I continued. "I just thank Him. I can't thank Him enough," he said.

I am sharing this because it captures who Professor Muller is. He may be one of the most brilliant and respected physicists and mathematicians, but he is also a lover of God, even though he is not sure who God is. He is also a very happy man who loves his family and loves life. He had just flown in from London where he had addressed the House of Lords. He must have been jet lagging, but seemed to really enjoy being

92

there with us. In fact, he seemed to be the type of person who would have enjoyed being just about anywhere, doing just about anything. I have met many scientists, and a few who are top in their field, but I had never met one who had this kind of profound joy in his life. I liked Professor Muller right away, but I still expected him to slice me to ribbons in our dialog.

The four of us sat around a small table with cameras facing us from all directions. When the taping began, I was asked to start and was told to take as long as I wanted to present my objections to the premise of man-made climate change. I had no idea that the next few hours would be some of the most invigorating, encouraging, and illuminating of the whole year. They would also raise my hope for science again.

The primary basis for my skepticism of man-made climate change was based on:

Problems with the science
Problems with the math
Problems with the psychology
Problems with the politics
Problems with the hypocrisy

I had a substantial basis for each of these. I had two notebooks full of studies and probably hundreds of files and articles on my laptop computer. Organizing them for this taping was a challenge, and presenting them was even more so. However, I felt an energy and flow that I knew was the

Helper with me. I started with the problems with the science and then went down the list. Following is a brief synopsis on each of the above categories that I covered.

The Science

For years, I have tried to read every article or study sent to me about climate change, especially those Anna sent. I had not yet found one that I thought was convincing, but rather the opposite. At best, I thought they were shallow and seemed to always include condescending digs at skeptics that I thought was very unscientific. Some were scary, seeming to reveal that science has fallen far from objectivity and reason. The more I read these, the more alarmed and skeptical I became. The fact that their models proved over and over to be so far off did not even seem to get their attention. Overall, I felt that something is fundamentally awry with the climate change premise, scientifically.

I went to the place where I knew I could get accurate climate models—Wall Street. They did not have a political dog in the fight. Their motive was that they had billions of dollars invested in commodities, and they wanted accuracy. Sure enough, the Wall Street models were far more accurate than any I found elsewhere.

Here I would like to insert a tiny climate science lesson. Climate changes have been happening since the earth was formed. One of the biggest factors in climate change is the result of the Atlantic and Pacific decadal oscillations. These are basically shifts in the ocean currents that cause such things as el Nino, which can radically impact weather all over the world. When the Artic ice cap started melting a few years ago, it was the result of the Gulf Stream shifting and going further east and north than usual. This is what really accounted for the rising temperatures in the artic waters, not CO2 in the atmosphere. When the Gulf Stream shifted back, the ice cap grew 40% in one year, which has been confirmed by both NASA and the European Space Agency, as they have been monitoring this from space.

When I began reading the articles and studies that challenged the premise of man-made climate change, they seemed to be on a much higher level of both reason and integrity. As stated, true science does not try to prove or disprove something, it finds the facts and lets them lead where they do. In my studies, this standard was sadly, and often alarmingly, lacking in the papers promoting man-made climate change. I had other problems with the science, but this was the basis that I presented, sharing a few of the more obvious examples. I also had articles by some of the most celebrated scientists who were far more articulate in their objections to man-made climate change.

The Math

I presented the articles about the NOAA having to shut down 600 reporting stations because the data was so flawed. They had been caught by the Government Accounting Office (GAO) taking temperature readings in asphalt parking lots, by steam vents, etc. This is nothing less than cooking the numbers. We know that people in the government do this with things such as economic reports, so this should not be a big surprise to us with something like climate change that has been so politicized. However, to this day it is hard to find a climate change proponent who even knows about this NOAA scandal. How are they being blinded to things like this?

On July 8, 2014 a front page story was carried in *The Globe* (London) explaining how the sea ice worldwide was over one million kilometers greater now than thirty-five years ago when they first began measuring the ice from satellites. The article included how the NOAA has continued to cook the numbers even after being caught by the GAO. They were actually using estimates from those stations that were forced to shut down because the data was so flawed. The numbers were purposely skewed to make it look like it was colder than it actually was thirty-five years ago and warmer now. This kind of thing is why climate change skepticism has grown in the U.K. by 800% in the last two years and is accelerating across Europe. This kind of thing not only erodes the confidence in U.S. science, but in the U.S. Government.

Al Gore's "hockey stick graph" was exposed for using seriously flawed basis points. This has been so widely exposed and debunked, even admitted by climate change believers that it is shocking that any climate change proponents are actually still using it. Instead, it is hard to find any who even know how these exaggerations have been revealed. You can do the best math in the world, but if you do not start with correct numbers, then your answer will be wrong.

I had a horde of studies with me, but only presented those that addressed the basics. However, it is an education to go back and watch *An Inconvenient Truth* by Al Gore to see how out of whack his projections were that are based on these numbers. The dates he used when the doom would hit have come and gone, and not even 10% of what was claimed actually happened. This is the result of seriously flawed data and a seriously flawed hypothesis. There are many other studies and articles that have proven to be just as awry.

Climategate (the exposing of emails by U.N. officials) actually included instructions on how scientists were to discard or change data that did not fit the climate change narrative. I understand that this is almost too shocking to believe, but the proof is there, and at least some of the authors of these emails admitted it. The narrative in the climate change advocate community is that Climategate has been debunked, but it was not debunked. It was covered up.

The Psychology

Again, you will see what you want to see, if you want to see it bad enough. That is why true science gets corrupted when experiments are done to find or prove a predetermined position. Much of this has happened with climate change, maybe more than in any previous "scientific" position in history.

Climategate also exposed the U.N. strategy for marginalizing, discrediting, and blackballing any scientist who expressed skepticism about man-made climate change. This is the most damning attack on science in recent times. There are now plenty of other accounts of scientists being refused grants, the universities they worked for losing grants, or threats of the same, if they expressed skepticism about climate change. The number of scientists coming out with this is still growing.

What could kill the objectivity required for true science more than things like the above coming down from governments? The truth has more dignity and strength than to use such base tactics. The tactics in *The Rules for Radicals* are still used by many to force their agendas, but this is the basis of totalitarian control. We must recognize it as a deadly enemy of the truth, including true science.

True religion can quickly become a cult when these kinds of tactics are used to control people. As Christians, we should be sensitive to this because of the multitudes of victims this has claimed throughout the church age, and even in our own time. Group-speak is one of the surest alarms that a lie or an evil agenda is being promoted or protected. This was the most troubling of all the issues I had with the man-made climate change agenda.

The Politics

Addressing this is like being a mosquito at a nudist colony: you know what you are there for but it's hard to know where to start. Whether politics has been corrupting science or science has been corrupting politics may be hard for some to tell, but I put my money on politics corrupting science.

It was a Republican President, Teddy Roosevelt, who was the first to make protecting the environment a political issue. Until President Obama another Republican, President Richard Nixon, was considered the best environmental President for his work creating the Environmental Protection Agency of the Federal Government. Even so, this should not be a political issue. When any agency of the government becomes a political pawn of one party or the other, there are terrible consequences. How climate change is being used in this way should be a case study for future generations.

We have briefly covered how liberals do not think that they can win an election without a crisis and how, therefore, Republicans doubt almost every crisis. If man-made climate change is real, then this is even more of a tragedy. This should be an issue seeking unity of purpose, not division.

I came with much ammunition on this corruption too, but only shared the principles and a few highlights in articles or studies, for the sake of time. However, how could anyone doubt the timing of the release of *Years of Living Dangerously* with the Obama Administration's thrust to make climate change his main political agenda? The American people are not as stupid as some assume. This kind of obvious coordination between Hollywood and the liberal agenda is starting to backfire.

With each of these, a volume of books could be written, but here I will try to give you an idea of how I addressed it. There is much more on the website if you want more sources and information. However, without question this is an issue that has been embraced almost exclusively on the left, with some from almost every political spectrum, even the far right, embracing it. Even so, most conservatives do not believe it, even though many of their reasons are as superficial as many who accept it thoughtlessly. The increasing number of skeptics are coming from independents, but again, this should not be determined by politics, but by science.

The Hypocrisy

Climate change activists exposed the fact that Al Gore's "carbon footprint" was more than twenty times what he was advocating for the rest of us. Those activists had their lives threatened by other activists for the damage this did to their cause. This all seemed to cause more skepticism not only because of Al Gore's hypocrisy, but also the extreme reactions and the lack of condemning these extreme reactions by any moderate voices in the climate change advocate community.

Another issue was when it was reported that Tom Steyer, one of President Obama's top environmental consultants and possibly the most active and vocal critic of the Keystone Pipeline, was found to be a major investor in the rival pipeline that would be built if Keystone was cancelled. The reports stated that he had already made a billion and a half in this investment and would stand to make billions more as soon as Keystone was tabled. This rival pipeline uses the same technology as Keystone, so it seemed in his thinking the only threat this was to the environment was if he was not an investor in it. It has also been widely reported that Steyer made at least part of his fortune as an investor in fossil fuels.

Steyer recently pledged $100 million in donations to candidates who fight climate change. Of course, this was rich fodder for conservatives who are now parading this news with Senate Democratic Leader Harry Reid's statement made from the Senate floor about the Koch Brothers, "What is un-American is when shadowy billionaires pour unlimited money into our democracy to rig the system...." What about Steyer? What about Soros? It seems Reid only thinks it is un-American if they are not contributing to Democratic campaigns.

I have traveled widely, and I often dialog with people in government and business leadership. I can say that this kind of highly visible corruption in our government, at the highest levels, now has the rest of the world viewing America like another banana republic. When the climate change issue gets mixed in with this kind of hypocrisy and corruption growing in politics, there is no thinking person who will not become more skeptical.

The Execution was a Good One

The above is a brief of what I shared that day, a brief of the basis for my objections. Since I had gone on for more than an hour, and I had much more, I felt to pause and give Professor Muller a chance to say something on any of these points. He had looked rather poker faced the whole time. I did not have any idea what he was thinking or what he would say. However, what he did say was completely unexpected.

He started by saying that he agreed with me on virtually every point. Then he went on to elaborate on many of the same things far more powerfully and articulately than I could have ever said it, and with far more evidence, scientifically analyzed, and presented with some brilliant charts he had with him.

I was absolutely astonished. This felt better than any "execution" I had ever been through. What most encouraged me was the brilliant and purely scientific objectivity, integrity, and reasoning evident in everything Professor Muller said. His charts were clear. His presentation was so engaging and full of insight that I could not help but think how wonderful it would have been to be one of his students at Berkeley.

Professor Muller had also been a climate change skeptic, and for more substantial reasons than I had. When he was offered a grant from the Koch Brothers to put together a team of the best scientists available to establish if there was any truth to climate change, he accepted. They tediously reconstructed the data, eliminating what had been gathered by fraudulent or questionable means. To their own astonishment, their research indicated that not only was climate change happening, but was indeed man caused.

However, what they also found was that the change was so minor and happening at such a slow rate that there was no reason for panic. The conclusion was that the earth's temperature had risen about six-tenths of a degree over the last half-century. At this rate, we had plenty of time to come up with solutions that would not cause more damage than the problem we were trying to fix. With the insight of a true scientific mind, he said the first thing we needed was to determine if this climate change was a bad thing or not.

I felt that this was the highest level of wisdom and reason I had yet come across in all of the studies I had waded through on this subject. Professor Muller had also done studies on such topics as what the impact would be if the United States completely stopped using fossil fuels. His conclusion was that the impact would be negligible because of all of the CO_2 being produced by China and India. If you throw in Russia, the rest of Asia, Africa, and South and Central America, then the impact of the United States completely ceasing to burn fossil fuels would hardly be measurable. He had brilliant charts to show this.

It was also Professor Muller's study that predicted the present cooling period that the world is experiencing. He foresaw it lasting about fifteen years, and then the gradual increase in temperature would begin again.

Anna, Ian, and I did not have much to say the rest of the day. I do not think any of us wanted to interrupt Professor Muller. I felt like I had found a national treasure. Ian said he wanted to take the Professor back home with him. It was the most inspiring day I had experienced in a long time, and it began to resurrect my hope for science.

Summary

Did I become convinced in man-made climate change? No. But I went from being close to a total denier, believing it was a complete sham, to being more open to it than when I began the project. I know everyone thought I was being incredibly stubborn, and maybe I was. However, there were still a few dots that had not connected for me. After all I had been through, I wanted to see the studies. Even so, many dots were connected for me, far more than I had hoped or expected.

Professor Muller had brought me one of his books, *Energy Policy for Future Presidents,* and I devoured it. I love science, but this is one of the best books I have ever read. This was not just because of the subject, but because of the refreshingly balanced and brilliant wisdom that flowed throughout. This book is a fresh breeze. It is full of the kind of wisdom and reason we are in desperate need of in these times.

Professor Muller and I started exchanging emails. I have become a major fan and believer in his work. Yet I have one major question on the evidence for man caused climate change that still has not been answered. I believe the conclusion that the temperature is rising *slightly*, and if we remove man's contribution from the equation, it does seem that it would not be rising at all. However, my question is, aren't we a part of nature too? Since the entire contribution of mankind to the CO_2

being put into the atmosphere is only 3½%, why is the burden entirely on mankind to reduce ours, if this is even needed?

I also have another thought, though it may be a stretch. I believe that the hand of God is helping us, even when we do not seem to want His help. For a long time, the big scare was that we were entering another ice age. Could it be that God having foreknowledge of this may be allowing fossil fuels and slight global warming as a way to prevent this ice age? I'm just sayin'...

It is understandable that the alarmism of the climate change agenda by itself makes many people skeptics. However, even if it is alarmism, and not true or only slightly true, there is some good that is coming from it. We need to consider how the things we do affect the planet. This is a basic Christian responsibility, and a basic human responsibility, as we are told in Psalm 115:16, **"The heavens are the heavens of the LORD, but the earth He has given to the sons of men."**

That is why God will not do things on the earth until we pray. He knows what we need better than we do, but He assigned the care of the earth to us. When He delegates, He does not recant even when we make a big mess of things. However, thankfully, we are assured that He will intervene before we completely destroy ourselves.

Now consider this. We are told that the Lord would return to save the earth or no flesh would survive (see

Matthew 24:22). Most have considered that this was because of the destructive weapons mankind has developed. Perhaps, but maybe we could consider that this is because of the way we are destroying the earth.

One of the concerns I have had since the beginning of the hysteria and exaggerations coming from the climate change community is the muddying of the waters to such a degree that the real issues and potentially more devastating ways we are polluting the earth are now being overlooked, or pushed to the back.

We have this crazy idea that science and faith are mutually contradictory. But anyone who really believes that must have a false idea of what science is—or a false idea of what faith is. Don't buy the science-versus-faith shtick. It's just not true.

- Eric Metaxas, *Everything You Always Wanted to Know About God, But Were Afraid to Ask*

9

The Three Great Questions

The account of Colonel Hal Moore that was played
by Mel Gibson in the film, *We Were Soldiers Once,* is
a true and remarkable story in U.S. military history.
One part that was left out of the movie was how Colonel Moore
was almost court-martialed after the epic battle portrayed in the
movie. Moore was accused of dereliction of duty for sleeping
during some of the most intense and dangerous parts of this
battle because he was leaning up against a termite mound with
his eyes closed. When questioned about this, he admitted to
doing this, but he was not sleeping. He was trying to shut out
the clamor of the battle to focus on three questions. When his
superiors learned what the three questions were, he was not
court-martialed, but commended. The three questions were then

added to the U.S. Army Manual to be used in confronting any crisis. They can help us to address this one as well. They are:

What is happening?
What is not happening?
What can I do about it?

I am now going to apply them to climate change from my own subjective perspective. If you have a different perspective you can still use this grid effectively for both understanding and taking action in this cause.

What is Happening?

Weather deals with the short-term changes in the atmosphere; climate is long-term. Weather can change almost instantly, or over a few hours, but climate changes much more gradually, taking years, decades, or even centuries. This is a natural process that has happened throughout history and will continue to happen. The issue is if exceptional or unnatural climate changes are occurring which are (or will be) detrimental to the eco stability of the earth, are they man caused and therefore preventable by man?

The causes of climate change can be varied, and like it or not, some of the main causes may yet remain hidden even from the best scientists. Science has made huge strides and the benefits are extraordinary, but it will always be imperfect because scientists are imperfect human beings like the rest of us. While science is making progress in understanding these matters, and their discoveries can be vital to our future, we still do not know all that can be known about climate.

Even if the present alarms from this have been somewhat extreme and hysterical, which is my present opinion, understanding climate, and any possible human affects on it, is a worthy devotion. If this is proven to be a fraud or an unnecessary "crying wolf," we must be careful not to overreact and throw the baby out with the bath water. Even learning this lesson will be helpful, but understanding climate could be one of the most important factors in our future.

Bottom Line

In my present opinion, Professor Richard Muller's study is the most credible I have seen. There is credible evidence that there has been a slight change in the earth's climate that could be attributed to man—a little over a half of a degree over the last half-century. This is not enough to cause panic, but is enough to get our attention.

We also have evidence that world temperatures have been decreasing over the last decade, not increasing. However, before we jump on that as evidence that global warming is not happening, the first scientific study that foresaw this decrease and predicted that it would last for over a decade was Professor

Muller's, which also concluded that man-made climate change is happening, but at quite a modest rate.

What is Not Happening?

Every storm, drought, flood, or disaster that happens is not being caused by climate change. The tendency of climate change proponents to use this kind of alarmism has taken a toll on their credibility. We can expect this to increase if they do not stop because it makes them appear ridiculous. There have been storms, droughts, floods, bad weather, and changing climates for millennium before mankind even knew there was such a thing as fossil fuels or CO2.

If climate change proponents try to use things like Hurricane Katrina or Hurricane Sandy as evidence, they are shooting themselves in the foot. Hurricanes Katrina and Rita were mega storms, and the year they hit was a violent hurricane season. However, since then we have enjoyed one of the longest and most quiet times in regard to hurricanes. A major cause for the increasing skepticism was that these storms did not keep getting bigger and more relentless as alarmists were predicting, making the lack of storms now appear as evidence that climate change is going away.

Of course, when Hurricane Sandy came and did damage, alarmists raised their voices again. Sandy was a large storm, but not very powerful. It only made it to a low Category II for a short time. Most of the damage was caused because it was moving so slowly, went over some extremely vulnerable places, and stayed over them through two high tides. Since Sandy, we have enjoyed another quiet time from storms.

Therefore, if these storms will be used as evidence that climate change is happening, then it must also be evidence that it has now stopped happening. You cannot have it both ways.

I was recently sent an article touting how accurate the climate change models have been. The only problem with this article is that they did not actually note which models they were referring to. The fact is that their models have been extremely inaccurate. According to Al Gore's "hockey stick" graphs, I am writing this from a beach house that is supposed to be about sixteen feet underwater now. Instead, the water is lower and the beaches wider than I remember ever seeing them. This has also been the testimony of the local fishermen. I'm just sayin'…

Regardless of what climate change advocates are saying, skepticism in climate change is growing around the world, and quickly, if you use real numbers. This may be a tragedy if climate change is real, but the alarmists would be to blame. Even if an alarm is called for, the messaging of this community has not been wise.

What Can We Do About It?

First, we need a panel of credible scientists, from all sides of the debate, without political bias, and devoted to the principles of true science, to conduct a credible study of what is actually happening with the climate.

Because of the loss of objectivity in so much of the climate sciences, "peer review" has also lost much of its credibility. This has too often been merely arranging those with credentials who already agree with you to add their endorsement to a study. Good science needs to encourage debate and challenge from every possible direction, just as all of the great theories are received. If the panel described above were convened, we would need to have their findings challenged in and with the highest principles of science to expose any possible flaws in them.

Secondly, if it is determined that man caused climate change is happening and it is, or is potentially, detrimental, then we need this panel, or another one with more specialized expertise, to propose actions. These would need to be presented, challenged, and debated according to the high principles of science, or we could end up with even worse problems.

Thirdly, it would be the place of governments to implement and enforce necessary actions, if needed.

As discussed, a major factor to consider is the tendency man has had to get partial knowledge of something and then start acting on it without understanding all of the consequences. Some of those actions have caused worse problems than the original ones we were trying to solve. We will likely be prone to keep making mistakes like this as long as we react in panic.

A good example of this would be the medical sciences. Certainly mankind has benefited from the advances there possibly more than in any other field. Even so, the trail to where we are now is littered with devastating procedures or products that hurt patients more, with remedies that sometimes caused problems worse than the diseases. These mistakes are still happening, as proven by the many TV legal advertisements for victims of these consequences.

The frequency of the above advertisements and the warning labels on almost every product now could make some people not want anything to do with modern drugs, medical products, or procedures. In truth, medical science is making remarkable progress even with the huge legal yoke it is carrying. We are foolish if we refuse to trust science at all, but we are just as foolish to put too much trust in it. Wisdom requires us to trust it to the degree that it has earned our trust. This should be true of how we relate to every science, including climate science.

Now if I believe in God's Son and remember that He became man, all creatures will appear a hundred times more beautiful to me than before. Then I will properly appreciate the sun, the moon, the stars, trees, apples, as I reflect that He is Lord over all things.

- Martin Luther

10

Science for Creation

In its formative years in the West, science grew under a heavy hand of oppression from the institutional church. Scientists who made discoveries that did not fit church dogma were often declared heretics, and the penalty for this was often death. This happened during the time when it was against the law to read The Bible. It was capital punishment for Christians to even be caught with a Bible. For this reason, it was not the Scriptures that were in conflict with science, but institutional, politically-driven dogma that was in conflict with it.

Of course, there have been many subsequent attacks on science by religious powers, and there have been many attacks on religion by scientists. Even so, with this history, can we blame science for its cynicism toward religion and the knee jerk reaction to keep religion out of the lab?

Just as you can have the best form of government but still have bad government if you have bad people in it, you can have true religion but have bad people leading it and using it for evil purposes. Likewise, the different sciences will be good or bad depending on the people leading them. We must learn to honor and receive good science and good scientists, and reject the bad. Scientists need to do the same with those of faith.

True science and true religion are the pursuit of the same thing—truth. For this reason, they should be best friends, allies, and co-laborers. Even though it still may not be popular to be in the field of science and admit to believing in a Creator, there is a substantial and growing movement in science to acknowledge that the evidence is overwhelming that this intricate, complex, interrelated, and interconnected environment could not have happened by accident. That implies a Creator, or at least an Initiator. Who that Creator may be varies from super aliens to Allah to the God of The Bible, but the evidence is so overwhelming that those who do not acknowledge this obvious fact are now starting to be considered awry.

Many scientists believe The Bible's account of creation is in basic conflict with scientific evidence about the age of the creation. That conflict lies more in the translations of The

Bible, and not in what The Bible actually says if you read it in the original languages in which it was written.

For example, the Hebrew word translated "day" in Genesis in relation to the creation is *yom,* which does not imply a twenty-four hour day, but rather an indefinite but distinct period of time. It could be translated day if you were using it like in "Napoleon's Day," but it could be translated more accurately "era." Whether these eras took place in hours or over millions of years is not clear in the original text, and so there is room to believe either without being in conflict with Scripture.

Neither does the use of the Hebrew word *yom* that was translated "day" imply that each of these days was the same length of time. One day could have been millions or billions of our years, while another not so long. It just means that during this era these things came forth in creation. There is a lot of science that supports this unfolding story of creation, including specific details included in Genesis such as a universal, worldwide flood.

Scripture also states that the seas were created from "the fountains of the deep," and refers to "springs from the deep" (see Genesis 7:11; 8:2). This has recently been confirmed by the discovery of subterranean "oceans" of water even larger than the surface oceans, and there are indications that our oceans came from these.

Even though religious dogma taught that the earth was flat for many centuries, the Scriptures refuted this, speaking of **"the circle of the earth" (see Isaiah 40:22).** This is a good example of how dogma can distort the teachings of Scripture, and how we need to be able to distinguish between the two.

If you believe in the Big Bang Theory of our beginning, which has been well confirmed as true, logic demands that you believe someone did the bang. This theory, now considered to be verified to five levels, which is exceptional with any theory, says that in one nanosecond there was nothing, and in the next nanosecond there was all of the matter and energy that is present in the universe. It is an impossible stretch to believe something like that happened without someone's engineering behind it.

Consider just this one aspect of the force of gravity: If it were stronger or weaker by the smallest measurable fraction (a point followed by forty zeroes), the universe could not exist. It would either fly apart or implode. Neither would it have been possible for matter to come together as planets, stars, or galaxies. The engineering of the physical universe was with a precision that is hard to even comprehend, much less duplicate.

If the speed of the expansion of the universe was the slightest bit different, either faster or slower, the universe would have either collapsed back on itself or flown apart. The perfect force of gravity enabled it to expand perfectly!

For either the force of gravity or the speed of expansion to happen by accident, it is said that the odds would be better for a tornado to hit a junk yard and leave behind a perfectly formed jumbo jet ready to carry passengers. Ray Hughes did say that he came from a town so poor that a tornado hit it and did six million dollars worth of improvements! Tornadoes are remarkable, but not a single tornado out of a zillion could make even a single Wright Flyer.

One scientist said that the odds of even a couple of the smallest miracles it took for the creation to come forth as it did would be like walking on the beach one morning and finding a brand new Mercedes with gas in the tank and keys in the ignition that the ocean had made the night before. You may protest that evolution takes millions, even billions of years, so though a Mercedes could not appear overnight, given enough time it could. I think we could give the ocean billions of years and it could not make a single tire. Science actually confirms this by the second law of thermodynamics, also known as the Law of Entropy.

Acknowledging the remarkable order to the creation that is infinitely beyond any human engineering, given time all of nature moves toward disorder, not order. Anything humans build, even with the best precision and engineering, will fall apart with time. Your car, your house, the space shuttle—even your human body starts falling apart over time. Even stars burn out, implode and explode over time. Nowhere in the creation can you find disorder that is proceeding toward order.

Therefore, the order that we have came from an outside influence. With outside influence such as maintenance, your car will last longer, as will your house, etc., but without it they will go toward disorder quickly. This has also proven true with social orders such as nations and cultures. They can have the best beginning, but without good maintenance they are going to proceed toward disorder and destruction.

For life to form, the sequential knowledge of a single strand of DNA is more of a miracle than the ocean making a Mercedes. When you take all of the perfect coincidences required for the creation to be what it is now, to even consider that nature did this on its own is fundamentally contrary to not only the Law of Entropy, but anything observed, which is supposed to be the basis of science. As William Paley (1743-1805) said, "Every watch requires a watchmaker." The order that exists in the universe is the work of someone. The real question with most of humanity, and increasingly with scientists, is "Who is the Watchmaker?"

One of the greatest scientists and thinkers of all time, Albert Einstein, was an atheist when he was young. As he grew in understanding, he became agnostic, and eventually he came to believe in the grand design of a Creator. I have not personally seen evidence that he ever determined who the

Creator was, but he called the intelligent design "the Reason" that manifests itself in all things.

Einstein's own General Theory of Relativity is what led him to believe in "the Reason"—God. When he developed this theory, he actually believed in a static universe, as most did at the time, which now seems almost as primitive as believing that the earth is flat. To make his theory work with a static universe, he had to throw in a "fudge factor" equation that did not make any sense, even to him. It actually required dividing by zero, which any third grader will tell you is not possible. When Hubble discovered the red shift and proved that the universe was expanding, Einstein went to the observatory himself to see it. This confirmed that the universe was expanding from a single point, and therefore had a beginning, and also a Beginner. At the time, this deeply troubled Einstein, but he was too intellectually honest to deny it.

Later Einstein called his "fudge factor equation" the greatest mistake of his life, but he was so resistant to the prospect of a Creator that he threw it in. That shows how far some will go to keep the God factor out of science. Thankfully there are many who, like Einstein, are too intellectually honest not to ultimately admit this mistake. Professor Richard Muller wrote to me that he did not believe in faith because you cannot do what he does and not see God, so you don't need faith because you have knowledge.

Those who claim that Einstein was an atheist are right, in one sense, as are those who claim he was agnostic, and too, those who claim that he believed in God. The truth is that he went through a process of discovery that led him closer and closer to God. People change as they mature, learn, and gain experience. There are people going through changes in their belief in man-made climate change or disbelief in it. How can both of these be true? Sometimes the process seems to be going in different directions, and may be, but it can still end up at the same place. If on both sides of this debate there are sincere seekers of truth, they will find the truth and be at the same place.

Many are troubled by politicians who convert from one party to the other. We should be skeptical when it is obviously merely political expedience to get on a winning side, but with some this is the result of expanded and maturing understanding. These we should trust more for their courage, not less.

Jesus warned about being an "old wineskin." An old wineskin cannot receive new wine because it is too rigid and inflexible. If the wineskin cannot expand, it will break. He was saying this as a metaphor about people. People become too rigid and inflexible to receive new ideas, but no disciple of Christ should be that way. We are called to be disciples, or students, throughout our whole life, continually growing and expanding in our understanding. We should not stop learning until we stop breathing. ⁄

I have met scientists who said it was their intent to prove that there was no God, and I've met scientists whose intent was to prove God. Neither of these are true science. True science does not have such an agenda, but has one agenda—to find the truth. To remain a true scientist, as I think Einstein is a great example of, you must be open to new ideas, and you must change your understanding with them. True science bases its conclusions on where the evidence leads, not on where we may want it to lead. Einstein resisted where his own theory was leading him for a time, but he was honest enough to finally admit the evidence. Can we?

Einstein would ultimately write, "Science without religion is lame; religion without science is blind." At first he wanted to find a loophole in his own greatest theory just to keep God out of it. As he matured, he understood how badly science and religion needed each other.

The great astronomer Robert Jastrow described himself as agnostic, but made some astounding statements about where the discoveries of science were leading, such as:

"Now we see how the astronomical evidence leads to the biblical view of the origin of the world. The details differ, but the essential elements in the astronomical and biblical accounts of Genesis are the same; the chain of events leading to man commenced suddenly and sharply at a definite moment in time, in a flash of light and energy."

Jastrow also wrote with amazing candor in his book, *God and the Astronomers:*

"For the scientist who has lived by his faith in the power of reason, the story ends like a bad dream. He has scaled the mountains of ignorance; he is the conqueror of the highest peaks; as he pulls himself over the final rock, he is greeted by a band of theologians who have been sitting there for centuries."

This is not to imply that there are not some conflicts between the teachings of The Bible and the accounts developed and accepted by many, and maybe even most, scientists. However, in almost all that I have come across in both fields, I have seen obvious bridges by which they could and should connect. They really are not that far from one another. The discoveries of science are regularly confirming biblical teachings, but only the scientists who know The Bible realize this. We Christians still need to get free of some of our Dark Age dogma and get back to what The Bible actually says in order to see it.

Spurgeon said that he could find ten men who would die for The Bible for every one man who would read it. There is evidence that there is even a smaller percentage of Christians who really know what The Bible says on basic and crucial issues. They believe what they do because someone who seemed wise and intelligent or someone they trusted told them. This may be okay for things that are not of great importance, but for the basics and for those matters of great importance, we must ourselves learn to follow the Spirit of Truth, Who "searches the depths" (see I Corinthians 2:10). No one who is truly Spirit led will be shallow in understanding.

Because **"God resists the proud, but gives grace to the humble" (see James 4:6)**, we must be careful not to let our increasing knowledge become a basis for pride and arrogance. It was for this reason that Jesus said babes would understand His truth before the wise and intelligent who had the truth hidden from them, seemingly by their pride in their own wisdom and intelligence (see Matthew 11:25). Babes tend to be humble and teachable, but they are also innocent, without an agenda. Such are the truly wise who will find the truth.

History repeatedly concurs that pride and/or other agendas have most often corrupted knowledge. Some Christians, who are actually ignorant of what a true Christian worldview is, can be the most dogmatic and wrong at times. The most dogmatic are usually those with the weakest foundations, which they can have even if they have ultimate truth on their side. So we should not write off a position just because overly zealous or dogmatic people are promoting it. However, that should be a caution for us.

Science is fighting many of the same battles that corrupted much of Christianity for so long. Some scientists can be experts in one field, but make dogmatic statements about fields they really do not have much knowledge of. That is a human trait, not just something scientists and Christians are guilty of. Maybe we can help science by admitting our mistakes, and thereby letting them learn from ours and not have to make their own.

To my Christian brothers and sisters, we must get engaged in this issue, and all of the other important issues of our time.

I would also like to recommend one of the best books on apologetics I have read, and one that I borrowed heavily from in this chapter for the quotes I used. *I Don't Have Enough Faith to be an Atheist,* by Norman L. Geisler and Frank Turek, is a page-turner and excellent for laying a healthy and solid foundational understanding of the relationship between science and faith.

Also, Frank hosts a regular program on the NRB television network titled, *I Don't Have Enough Faith to be an Atheist*, on which he addresses many of the scientific, philosophical, and cultural fault lines of our time.

For further study, you may access my source studies on the climate change debate with this link: **www.theoakinitiative. org/climate-change**

Appendix A:

An Open Letter to My Daddy Who Doesn't Accept Climate Change

Posted: 05/02/2014 11:42 am EDT
Updated: 05/02/2014 1:59 pm EDT

*This poignant letter is to my father, who is among the most powerful evangelical ministers in the world. Pastor Rick Joyner heads MorningStar Ministries, a global group with over 100 churches and partners in dozens of countries. My father won't accept that climate change is human-caused. In this Sunday night's episode of **Years of Living Dangerously**, Showtime at 10 p.m., I take him to meet scientists and see the situation on the ground. I wrote this open appeal to him.*

Dear Daddy,

As you know, combating climate change is my life's work. I believe it is the greatest challenge of our time. I feel a deep duty, to both my faith and my generation, to spread this message. We are the first generation that knows how serious the stakes are, as well as the last to be able to do something about it in time.

I learned from you that we are called on to protect God's creation and to love our neighbors. I write you today because we need your leadership to achieve a bright future for all of us—and our children.

Fossil fuels have brought the world many wonderful things, but now we know they come with a high price— an unimaginably high price if we don't act soon to start transitioning off of them. We need to create a world where our energy needs are met without depending on fossil fuels that make us sick and heat up our planet. We can only do this together.

Daddy, I know you are someone who takes stewardship of creation as a moral mandate. I believe ignoring climate change is inconsistent with our faith. The risks are massive, and the science is clear. If we do nothing, our planet will face severe impacts, and billions of people will be hurt, most of whom contributed little or nothing to the problem. How is that just? How is that loving our neighbors?

Many people are already being negatively impacted, such as our friends, the oystermen, in Apalachicola, along with people from Texas to Bangladesh, from Syria to Staten Island—whose powerful stories are told in the Showtime series you and I appear in, *"Years of Living Dangerously."*

It's not just livelihoods at stake, it is our lives, God's greatest gift to us. Daddy, will you use your voice to be a part of the solution? Christians are believers in resurrection, renewal, and salvation, even against all odds. We can help bring much needed light and healing to this situation, or we can allow misinformation and myopia to continue to be a hurdle to hope.

You are right, we do need truth. And now, more than ever, we also need action. I hope you'll join me in working to overcome this great challenge, maybe the greatest our planet has ever faced. You and I both know our faith has risen to the occasion before and overcome great injustice and incredible obstacles. I hope we can come together, and do it now for our planet and for each other.

Love you,
Anna Jane

Some people, in order to discover God, read books. But there is a great book: the very appearance of created things. Look above you! Look below you! Read it. God, whom you want to discover, never wrote that book with ink. Instead, He set before your eyes the things that He had made. Can you ask for a louder voice than that?

- St. Augustine

Appendix B:

An Open Letter to My Daughter Who I Disagree With About Climate Change

Dear Anna,

Though I may not be convinced of manmade climate change, I do share the belief in the basic responsibility mankind has for protecting the creation. I would be a hypocrite to be pro-life and not be for all life. I consider it a great human failure and tragedy for any life to be lost, hurt, poisoned, or to have their environment polluted, because of our greed, selfishness, or irresponsibility. I am very proud of you for fighting such a good fight for all of the living creatures who cannot fight for themselves against this irresponsibility. This fight is for man as well.

As the word "conservation" comes from conservative, I am thankful for you helping me and many of my conservative friends to be more deeply reminded of this basic mandate. I love the creation because it is so awesome and deserving of our love and protection. I also love it because I love the Creator who gave us such an awesome gift as a home. To disrespect this gift is to disrespect the Giver.

I also deeply love and appreciate science. I believe science is the result of another remarkable gift from our Creator—intelligence and curiosity. I am thankful to science for all of the ways it has enriched our lives and made them easier, safer, and more enjoyable. It is out of a love for science, not a refutation of it, that I remain a climate change skeptic.

Much of the science behind climate change has been so exaggerated, distorted, and in other ways flawed to the degree that it insults and attacks the very foundations of true science—which is skepticism, challenge everything, and promote debate, never cutting it off. True science does not pursue knowledge to prove a position but rather to find the truth.

That being said, there are many Christians who have in the same ways, and out of their zeal, corrupted the truths they were trying to promote about Christianity. The pressure to conform caused compliance with dogma to eclipse the love of the truth for much of our history. Even so, the truths of Christianity are true even if immature and unsavory people have often caused problems for Christianity with their strong, but misguided zeal. For this reason, I remain a climate change skeptic, and not a denier. There is a difference. I remain open to it, but not convinced. I'm not convinced because the waters are still so muddied. I remain open because this has happened to virtually all important truths.

Besides the science, the math, the psychology, the politics (and I could go on), one of the primary causes of my doubt about this is the seeming inability of climate change proponents to even listen to the other side. Truth is strong enough not to overreact to challenges, but embrace them and openly consider them. True science is built on such openness to challenges and debate. There are many legitimate scientists who are not only climate change skeptics, but also troubled by what they see as the corruption of science by the climate change hysteria as they refer to it.

Though I think the extremes in every movement often hurt those movements the most, I am very thankful for the environmentalists who have done so much to help clean up our rivers, our oceans, and our land, and to protect the creatures who cannot speak for themselves. I know there is much more to be done in this, and I hope to always be a part of this worthy cause. I am also very proud of you for your devotion to this, and want to help you every way I can, but I would not be helping you if I ever compromised my convictions without being convinced they are wrong. I pray that you have this same resolve even though at times we may have different convictions about some things.

Your Proud Father,

Rick Joyner

Appendix C:

Letter From An Agnostic

Dear Sir,

I was impressed, and that is not easy for an agnostic, at your dedication to your daughter in a recent episode I had recorded of *Years of Living Dangerously*. I realize it took an incredible amount of fortitude and wisdom to allow such an endeavor.

I am no scholar on gods, prophets, or writings of such matters, but I can recognize when one of the greatest of human potentials is being cultivated—that of the open mind. The show indicated that you had the incredible patience to pursue, for ten years, a discussion of global warming with your daughter; coming all the way from stopping funding for such education of her to allowing her to speak to your congregation. I mentioned that I am no profound person of any god's anointing, but I have been compelled to write to you.

I believe if there is a god, and he calls on shepherds such as yourself, that he would expect the highest order of thought and action on your part. Your recent ability to open yourself to explore the possibilities that humans may indeed be a factor in the changing of our global climate is of the highest degree in human, let alone religious example that one could aspire to. If you think about the place you are at, the multitudes that believe in your every word, you sir, are in a very high order of thought evolution; for a large many, you present the world as they see it.

I must say also, you now represent to me the hope for synthesis in those like myself and your followers' faith; the stitched fabric of both believers and skeptics. If you truly believe you are doing the work for an incredibly superior being or entity, then you have recently been called to the highest post of stewardship.

I watched in fascination and excitement as you were gracious enough to speak with obvious leaders in both the scientific and religious fields on the matter. Your leadership is forming now, and I wish you great clarity of mind to help in the effort to save an amazing wonder we call home and you call God's creation. I believe if there is a god, he awaits your report. I know your recent intellectual exploration would be highly commended by a superior being.

So many need your guidance and I am cheering you on in the struggle to explain to the world that indeed humans are not always perfect and that we may have tipped the balance. It is not a slight against any deity here; for sure, such divinity could only applaud the highest of human thoughts. I simply want to thank you for allowing the story to be told. I would love to speak with you, if at all possible, on the matter.

Please feel free to write and discuss anything. I wish you all the best in your leadership for good.

Thank You.

The creation is quite like a spacious and splendid house, provided and filled with the most exquisite and the most abundant furnishings. Everything in it tells us of God.

- John Calvin

Years of Living Dangerously: Pastor Rick Joyner Models Feynman's Ideal Scientist!

By Jim Steele, Director Emeritus Sierra Nevada Field Campus, San Francisco State University

Richard Feynman idealized the good scientist as someone who displays "a kind of scientific integrity, a principle of scientific thought that corresponds to a kind of utter honesty—a kind of leaning over backwards. For example, if you're doing an experiment, you should report everything that you think might make it invalid—not only what you think is right about it: other causes that could possibly explain your results; and things you thought of that you've eliminated by some other experiment, and how they worked—to make sure the other fellow can tell they have been eliminated."

In Episode 4 of *Years of Living Dangerously* while attempting to depict his resistance to "their science," the producers inadvertently revealed that it was only climate skeptic Pastor Rick Joyner who truly practiced Feynman's ideal.

In contrast, the documentary's producers demonstrated how one-sided political consensus building is practiced to evoke climate alarm. While Pastor Joyner leaned over backwards to understand his daughter's global warming concerns, the documentary failed to report the science that might make the CO_2 connection *invalid*. While Joyner embodies Albert Einstein's advice to "Never Stop Questioning," the documentary tries to subtly denigrate his questioning as a stubborn refusal to believe what the alarmists were preaching. In gross contrast to America's public schools where coordinated efforts teach students how to resist peer pressure and think for themselves, the documentary offered no scientific discussion. They simply demonstrated that consensus is built via heavy peer pressure.

The documentary exploited the struggles of Apalachicola Bay's oyster fishermen who have recently watched their oysters disappear as the bay has become increasingly saline due to low flows in the Apalachicola River. Pastor Joyner willingly boards 2 fishermen's boat to witness the absence of oysters in their hauls, and then the documentary implies that it was

CO2 climate change at the root of the fisherman's suffering. Although sympathetic to the fishermen's plight, Pastor Joyner maintained his skepticism, and his stance is supported by most scientific studies.

Although the narrator briefly mentioned the fact that reduced flows in the Apalachicola River were partly due to increased upstream diversions, we never witness anyone sharing or discussing this alternative viewpoint with the pastor. Nor is anyone informed that during an earlier cool phase of the Pacific Decadal Oscillation, the droughts of the 1950s brought even less precipitation to the region, yet there was still greater river flow and less damage to the bay's fisheries. In a 2008 report "Importance of River Flow to the Apalachicola River-Bay System"[1] scientists reported, "A cumulative deficit evaluation of the drought events showed that the greatest cumulative rainfall deficit occurred during the mid 1950s drought event, but the greatest flow deficit occurred during the 1999–2002 drought event." The report warned, "With permanent reductions of Apalachicola River flow in the region related, in part, to reservoir and other recent water management practices, the adverse effects of natural droughts would be accentuated."

If the documentary wanted to educate the public about the best practices of science, they would have examined all the facts including well-known water management practices. But only Pastor Joyner seemed willing to explore such alternative viewpoints. The producers efforts would have done more good if they had tried to enlist the pastor's influence to promote better watershed management. But the producers seemed intent on bending over backwards to suggest recent droughts were unnatural and caused by rising CO_2. Our best scientists do not support that suggestion either.

Regarding the droughts that affected the river's flow, the NOAA Drought Task Force had reported that "the prior year's southern plains drought that spanned October 2010-August 2011, existed owing to a strong sensitivity of that region to La Niña conditions." In contrast, the ocean surface patterns gave no warning of the looming 2012 drought, and climate scientists determined that year's drought was "an event resulting largely from internal atmospheric variability having limited long lead predictability" [2]

The NOAA Drought Task Force concluded, "Climate simulations and empirical analysis suggest that neither the effects of ocean surface temperatures nor changes in greenhouse gas concentrations produced a substantial summertime dry signal over the central Great Plains during 2012."

Drought always causes higher temperatures, but curiously they also reported that given the lack of rainfall, the high temperatures were not as high as expected writing, "The scatter plot shows that 2012 was the driest summer in the historical record, though the temperature anomaly of +2°C was exceeded by two prior summers—1934 and 1936. Indeed, although the 2012 summer experienced less rainfall over the central Great Plains than in either 1934 or 1936, those years were about 0.5°C warmer." Such observations contradict what we would predict if the region had been experiencing the additive effects of CO2 warming. That is likely due to the fact that the southeastern USA has been a "warming hole"[3] that experienced a slight cooling trend between 1895 and 2007 even after climate scientists questionably adjusted the data as discussed in "Unwarranted Temperature Adjustments: Conspiracy or Ignorance?"

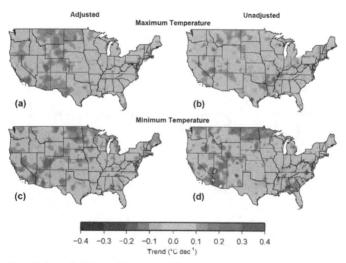

Figure 13. Geographic distribution of linear trends in HCN version 2 temperatures for the period 1895 to 2006. Areas in white indicate trends in excess of 0.4°C dec⁻¹: (a) adjusted maximum temperatures; (b) unadjusted maximum temperatures; (c) adjusted minimum temperatures; (d) unadjusted minimum temperatures.

Instead of discussing all the science, the producers try to bludgeon Pastor Joyner with Christian peer pressure beginning with his daughter. Then Katherine Hayhoe visits and repeats the same simplistic arguments from Episode 1. Then former U.S. Representative Bob Inglis piles on. Finally Pastor Joyner is brought to Dr. Richard Muller who has been hailed as the Koch-brothers-funded skeptic who now believes in CO_2-caused warming. But the producers fail to mention that Muller's homogenized instrumental data may suffer from the same biases illustrated in "Unwarranted Temperature Adjustments: Conspiracy or Ignorance?" Or contrasting satellite data that shows the global average has not risen in 17 years.

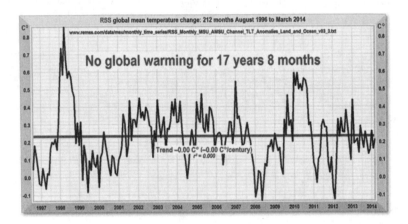

Or that not one tree ring study (from locations where temperatures are not influenced by urbanization effects) supports Muller's interpretation of rapidly rising temperatures. A paper by 10 of the world's top dendrochronologists reported, "No current tree ring based reconstruction of extra-tropical

Northern Hemisphere temperatures that extends into the 1990s captures the full range of late 20th century warming observed in the instrumental record."[4] In contrast to Muller's reconstructions, a majority of the tree ring studies show a slight cooling since the 40s, despite the rise in temperature during the 80s and 90s. This has been called the "divergence problem."

Nor do the producers discuss with Pastor Joyner about Muller's dubious suggestion that his reconstruction of the global average since the 1850s was due to CO2. Most climate scientists do not believe CO2 had a significant impact until after the 1950s. For example when discussing the abrupt warming in the Arctic from the 1920s to 40s, Sweden's top climate scientist and IPCC member Lennart Bengtsson wrote: "It seems unlikely that anthropogenic forcing on its own could have caused the warming, since the change in greenhouse gas forcing in the early decades of the twentieth century was only some 20% of the present. Second, it remains to be explained the marked cooling trend between 1940 and 1960, a period with a similar or faster increase of the greenhouse gases than between 1920 and 1940".

As data accumulates, Bengtsonn has become more skeptical but his shift to skepticism has not gotten the same media fanfare as Muller. Bengtsonn has become increasingly upset by the IPCC's attempt to force a consensus, similar to the tactics employed by *Years of Living Dangerously* against Pastor Joyner.

In a recent interview here Dr. Bengtsonn's wrote, "I believe the whole climate consensus debate is silly. There is not a single well-educated scientist that question that greenhouse gases do affect climate. However, this is not the issue but rather how much and how fast. Here there is no consensus as you can see from the IPCC report where climate sensitivity varies with a factor of three! Based on observational data climate sensitivity is clearly rather small and much smaller that the majority of models".

The episode interspersed segments of applying peer pressure to Pastor Joyner, with 60 Minutes' Lesley Stahl who visits Greenland to suggest rising CO2 has created unusual changes there. But Stahl failed to do her homework or ask the probing questions that 60 Minutes was once known for. For example, she never asked about the research from climate scientists at Los Alamos National Laboratories who concluded: **"We find no direct evidence** to support the claims that the Greenland ice sheet is melting due to increased temperature caused by increased atmospheric concentration of carbon dioxide. **The rate of warming from 1995 to 2005 was in fact lower than the warming that occurred from 1920 to 1930"** [6] (emphasis added).

As seen in their graph, Greenland temperatures show a more cyclical nature with more warmth in the 30s and 40s and in agreement with most tree ring studies.

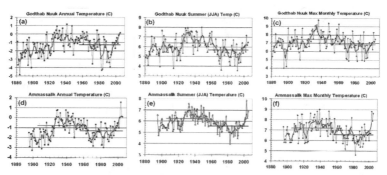

Figure 2. (a and d) Records of an annual average, (b and e) summer months (June, July and August) average, and (c and f) the warmest month of a year temperature at Godthab Nuuk and Ammassalik. Solid black curve is a five-year running average, red horizontal line is a 1905–1955 average and horizontal blue line is a 1955–2005 average temperature. All temperature data used are from the NASA GISS website.

The retreat of Greenland's glaciers has been largely due to intruding warm waters driven by changes in natural ocean oscillations. Those ocean oscillations increased the flow of warm Gulf Stream waters that eventually bathe the coast of Greenland and islands in the Arctic Ocean. Those warm currents melted the bottoms of any glaciers that terminated in the ocean.

Greenland's largest outlet glacier, Jakobshavn Isbrae, drains about 7% of the Greenland ice sheet and generates 10% of the Atlantic's icebergs. During the Holocene Optimum beginning about 9000 years ago, Jakobshavn retreated further than its present day terminus and remained that way for almost 7,000 years. It was only recently during the Little Ice Age that Jakobshavn rapidly advanced several kilometers beyond today's terminus.[7]

The North Atlantic Oscillation and Atlantic Multidecadal Oscillation's influences on warm ocean currents explain both Greenland's cyclical temperature behavior and current glacial retreat. The glaciers' **most rapid 20th century retreat occurred between 1920 and 1950**, followed by an advance in the 1970s and then a renewed retreat in 1998[7,8,9] (emphasis added).

The rapid retreat of Jakobshavn between 1920 and 1940, as well as in the 1990s, corresponds to North Atlantic regime shifts during which warm waters from the Atlantic were pushed into the Arctic. Marine biologists wrote, "The warming in the 1920s and 1930s is considered to constitute the most significant regime shift experienced in the North Atlantic in the 20th century."[10] Fishery biologists observed that "species of fish such as cod, haddock, and herring expanded farther north while colder-water species such as capelin and polar cod retreated northward. The maximum-recorded movement involved cod, which spread approximately 1200 km northward along West Greenland." The warm water and associated species lingered for 2 more decades before retreating in the 1960s.

We are all blinded by our illusions and we can only free ourselves from those illusions by careful observations, experiments, and respectful debate. I was brought up in a devout Christian family but I am no longer a churchgoer. My parents and I differed on the concepts of evolution. However, I still embrace their ideals embodied in the Golden Rule and Abraham's devotion to knowing the greater truth. Abraham's willingness to sacrifice his son to be closer to God is religion's equivalent of Feynman's ideal scientist who leans over backwards to prove that he has not been fooled by clinging to a cherished belief. Pastor Joyner embodied the best of his religion and science. He willingly ventured into the wilderness of climate alarmism and respectfully listened to a parade of opposing viewpoints. He allowed his daughter to share her opposing beliefs to his congregation. He demonstrates his faith that only the truth will set you free.

Compare Pastor Joyner's actions to those of prominent global warming alarmists and ask who best demonstrates the integrity of Feynman's ideal scientists and the pursuit of truth. Compare Pastor Joyner's openness to David Suzuki's demand that society "Deny the Deniers the Right to Deny." Or top CO2 climate scientist Kevin Trenberth's Joint Presidential Session on Communicating Climate Change speech titled "Communicating Climate Science And Thoughts On Climategate" when he advises fellow scientists to act contrary to scientific ideals. Branding skeptics as deniers he condescends, "Debating them about the science is not an approach that is recommended. In a debate it is impossible to counter lies, and caveated statements show up poorly against loudly proclaimed confident statements that often have little or no basis." And in the published versions provides a cartoon proclaiming skeptics are the world's greatest threat.

Accordingly, climate alarmists have circled the wagons and refused to debate with climate skeptics, preferring hit pieces such as *Years of Living Dangerously*. Climate modeler Gavin Schmidt and Michael Mann's sidekick on the RealClimate website, would only appear on John Stossel's show if there was no face to face debate and skeptic scientist Dr. Roy Spencer removed himself while Schmidt was on stage. And Michael Mann, the creator of the hockey stick interpretation of climate change not only calls everyone who disagrees with his viewpoint a denier but anti-science. But it is only via thorough skeptical examination that challenges every hypothesis does a scientific opinion become trustworthy. However, climate alarmists like Mann demean any and all who question CO_2 as deniers, as if the truth has been already determined. They promote their view on websites and op-ed pieces encouraging a new intellectual tyranny aimed at shutting down all skeptics.

I suggest they will be better scientists if they emulated Pastor Joyner, and listen to all sides, promote more debate, and then let the truth lead us wherever it may.

Cited Scientific Literature that supports
Pastor Joyner's Skepticism

1. Livingston (2008) Importance of River Flow to the Apalachicola River-Bay System.

   Report to the Florida Department of Environmental Protection
   http://mayorvanjohnson.com/files/Livingston_Report.pdf

2. An Interpretation of the Origins of the 2012 Central Great Plains Drought

   Assessment Report. NOAA Drought Task Force.
   http://drought.gov/media/pgfiles/2012-Drought-
   Interpretation-final.web-041013_V4.0.pdf

3. Menne. M., (2009) The U.S. Historical Climatology Network Monthly Temperature Data, version 2. The Bulletin for the American Meterological Society. p. 993-1007

4. Wilson (2007) Matter of divergence: tracking recent warming at hemisphcric scales using tree-ring data. Journal of Geophysical Research–A, 112, D17103, doi: 10.1029/2006JD008318.

5. Bengtsson, L., et al., (2004) The Early Twentieth-Century Warming in the Arctic—A Possible Mechanism. Journal of Climate, vol. 445-458

6. Chylek, P., et al. (2006) Greenland warming of 1920–19 30 and 1995–2005. Geophysical Research Letters, vol. 33, L11707, doi:10.1029/2006GL026510

7. Young, N., et al., (2011) Response of Jakobshavn Isbræ, Greenland, to Holocene climate Change. Geology, vol. 39, p. 131-134.

8. Motyka, R., et al. (2010) Submarine melting of the 1985 Jakobshavn Isbræ floating tongue and the triggering of the current retreat. Journal of Geophysical Research, vol. 116, F01007, doi:10.1029/2009JF001632

9. Csatho, B., et al., (2008) Intermittent thinning of Jakobshavn Isbræ, West Greenland, since the Little Ice Age. Journal of Glaciology, vol. 54, p. 131-145.

10. Drinkwater, K. (2006) The regime shift of the 1920s and 1930s in the North Atlantic. Progress in Oceanography vol. 68, p.134–151.

Greenland discussion adapted from the chapter *"Many Ways to Shrink a Glacier" in Landscapes & Cycles: An Environmentalist's Journey to Climate Skepticism*

Read previous essays at **landscapesandcycles.net**

Jim Steele

In 1983, San Francisco State University's biology department wanted to close the Sierra Nevada Field Campus and use the savings to support more molecular and genetic research. Although Jim Steele was just completing his Masters Degree, Dean Kelley believed Jim Steele was the best person to resurrect and grow the Sierra Nevada Field Campus. Together they turned the rustic Sierra Nevada Field Campus into one of California's leading environmental education centers. He was also the principal investigator for the Sierra Nevada Neotropical Migratory Bird Riparian Habitat Monitoring project sponsored by the U.S. Forest Service and that research prompted the restoration of the Carman Valley Watershed.

His understanding of climate change evolved as he sought to understand the causes of the declines in local bird populations which he studied each summer as part of the Sierra Nevada Neotropical Migratory Bird Riparian Habitat Monitoring project. Believing the politics of global warming have been misguiding conservation efforts, Jim Steele wrote the book, *Landscapes & Cycles: An Environmentalist's Journey to Climate Skepticism.* For more information, visit: **www.landscapesandcycles.net**

MorningStar TV.com

ON DEMAND

Watch Your Favorite Speakers and Worship Leaders at MorningStar TV

**Sunday Services • School of the Spirit
MorningStar Conferences • Featured Videos
Special Webinars • PPTV • And More**

Large video archive ▪ Stream on your mobile device
Enjoy DVD quality picture ▪ Easy to navigate

www.MorningStarMinistries.org